ONE AT A TIME:

THE LIFE, PASSION, AND ONGOING GLOBAL IMPACT OF LARRY WARD

Please enjoy this story of our Founder.

Dick

ISBN 978-0-692-39622-3

Copyright © 2015 Food for the Hungry

All rights reserved

Printed in the United States of America

… **ONE AT A TIME:**
THE LIFE, PASSION, AND
ONGOING GLOBAL IMPACT
OF LARRY WARD

NORMAN B. ROHRER

Food for the Hungry
Phoenix, Arizona

TO THE POOR IN A RICH WORLD

CONTENTS

1	A DIFFERENT WORLD	**11**
2	WHAT'S HE REALLY LIKE	**15**
3	"FACT, FAITH, FEELING . . ."	**25**
4	SACRED JOYS OF HOME	**33**
5	GOAL TO GO	**37**
6	INTO THE BRAZEN THROAT OF WAR	**41**
7	A HOME AND CAREER	**45**
8	GOD'S SYNCHRONY	**51**
9	WORLD VISION	**61**
10	BOB PIERCE	**71**
	PHOTOGRAPHS	**75**
11	"IF YOU DRAW OUT YOUR SOUL TO THE HUNGRY . . ."	**79**
12	"THEY DIE ONE AT A TIME . . ."	**85**
13	A LIFELONG LOVE AFFAIR	**97**
14	"WHERE ONLY MAN IS VILE"	**103**
15	THE THREE	**111**
16	LET MY PEOPLE GO!	**123**

17	"PROJECT NOAH"	**133**
18	HIS BROTHER'S KEEPER	**137**
19	"GOD DID SEND A SHIP"	**143**
20	THANK GOD FOR A SENSE OF HUMOR	**149**
21	BEYOND	**159**
	AFTERWORD: THE GROWTH AND FUTURE OF FOOD FOR THE HUNGRY	**163**
	THE WHITE HOUSE	**171**

Wherever I am,
though far away
at the ends of the earth,
I will cry to you
for help.

PSALM 61:2

from the flyleaf of
Larry Ward's Living Bible

FORETHOUGHTS

F EW MEN are as strong, need less sleep, can read as fast, have traveled as many miles, have seen as much suffering, as Lawrence Edward Ward; but the theme of this book focuses on none of the above. This is the record of a man tenanted by love, joy, and worship, a man with the courage to trust God in the paragraphs as well as in the chapters of his work.

In 1957, when I met Larry in Los Angeles I knew that a treasured friend had entered my presence. That chance meeting altered the course of my life. I hope this encounter will do the same for you.

Since that meeting, I have worked with him in various editorial positions, listened to him preach, read his reports about God's earth-wide enterprise, laughed at his artful and diplomatic wit, felt his shoulder-bruising welcome-home hug (a leftover from college wrestling), joined his Skippers Anonymous Club ("joggers never look like they're having fun"), watched him pray for the emaciated and dying, joined him in the halls of the mighty, and became a supporter of the relief and development projects of Food for the Hungry, which he founded.

Is he perfect? Following the first interview for this book Larry wrote a note incorporating Lincoln's words to his portraitist: "Leave the warts in." Larry is sometimes criticized by judgmental Americans for his metabolism that has turned from thickset into paunchy. He can sing off-key, detests mice, suffers from loneliness when absent from his wife and children, can be angered by the tyranny of little minds or by an associate who dismisses a problem as insoluble, and fears taking credit for godsends.

Larry's affirmations come not alone from his peers, or from a book, but rather from the impoverished of the world whom God delivered because, as did the psalmist, this man cried and God heard him and delivered many out of all their troubles.

Dietrich Bonheoffer described Jesus Christ as "the man for others." I think of Larry Ward, the Lord's servant, in corresponding terms.

NORMAN B. ROHRER

INTRODUCTION (2015)

THE STORY that unfolds in the coming pages recounts the amazing life and faithfulness of Dr. Larry Ward, the founder and first president of Food for the Hungry, an organization that currently serves over 9.5 million people in over twenty countries and is still actively working to end poverty in some of the most vulnerable areas of the world. This book, originally titled, *This Poor Man Cried*, was written by Larry Ward's friend and associate, Norman B. Rohrer, and was first published in 1984 by Tyndale House Publishers. It has been updated to reflect the incredible impact that Food for the Hungry has made on global poverty in recent times and the dire necessity of the organization's continued assignments. The mission of Food for the Hungry, including its core principles, is still very much driven by the vision, the unwavering faith in God's provision, and the often larger-than-life (but true) stories of its founding president.

That vision can be traced back to 1970, when God began to intensify a burden for the world's most at-risk people in the heart of Dr. Ward. Having worked at World Vision for several years in the 1960s, the former editor of *Christianity Today* had witnessed first-hand the dire realities and extreme plight of the poor from all around the world. One evening, he dreamed he was looking into the faces of 12,000 people all dying of starvation. Ward would express the profound calling that God had placed on his heart with moving clarity: *"About all I could do in my prayer was admit to God that the great overwhelming burden for a hungry world—which so long and so slowly had been forming in my heart and mind—had now suddenly crystallized into something specific, sharp, prodding."* Larry did the only thing he could think of, which was to kneel down beside his bed and pray, *"Here am I, Lord, send me."*

So in September 1970, Larry Ward resigned from his place at World Vision at the age forty-five to begin a new career with a single focus and the desperate mission of feeding starving people. On a trans-Pacific flight, Larry (along with his twelve-year old son Kevin), was inspired by their reading of Psalm 146:7, "*He upholds the cause of the oppressed and gives* **food to the hungry**." Less than a year later, in January 1971, the first Board of Directors was assembled, and Food for the Hungry was established in the United States.

Moved by a broken heart from seeing the reality of a hungry world and inspired to action by the Word of God, Ward hoped that Food for the Hungry could become an *international* body comprised of organizations reaching out to help the poor, in his words, "one person at a time." Early in his ministry, he had prayed, "Father, what can I do? I'm just one person." God responded to Larry Ward with a clear and audible answer, **"But they die one at a time… so we can help them one at a time. And we must."** God's vivid answer to Larry's prayerful question would become an encouragement for the many who would come after him. Food for the Hungry would always remain grounded in the divine truth that one person *can* make a difference. Even after its initial decade of ministry (just several years before the first publication of *This Poor Man Cried*), Food for the Hungry had quickly proven God's faithfulness to their mission by impacting the world far beyond what one person could do alone in the battle against hunger and poverty.

In 1980, the first step toward Larry Ward's continued vision of an *international* body became a reality with the founding of Food for the Hungry International (FHI) in Geneva, Switzerland. The mission would expand exponentially to implement unified relief and development programs in locations all over the world through an international partnership of supporting national organizations or affiliates. Consequently, Japan International Food for the Hungry (JIFH) was established just a year later in 1981.

In 1984, Larry Ward decided it was time to step down as the president of the mission organization that God had planted in his heart. But, the mission that had grown from his compassion continued to flourish. Today, Food for the Hungry has served the poor of the world for over 45 years. Throughout that time, the world has changed and along with it the needs and challenges of the very people that Food for the Hungry has remained steadfastly committed to serving. After Ward's departure, God continued to provide (in His own perfect timing) remarkable leaders such as Dr. Ted Yamamori, Ben Homan, and today's CEO Gary Edmonds. Each are uniquely gifted to help Food for the Hungry to effectively address the latest global challenges of the poor and oppressed. No matter the incarnation of leadership, Food for the Hungry has throughout its history, remained steadfastly grounded in the vision God imparted to its founding president, Dr. Larry Ward.

To appreciate the dramatic impact and distinctive mission of this remarkable organization, it is true that you must first understand the extraordinary life and unshakeable faith of its organizer. The current President of Food for the Hungry, Gary Edmonds, speaks in reverent terms about the eternal impact of Dr. Ward's life on the poor and oppressed of our 21st century world, "Larry's spirit is at the very foundation of Food for the Hungry. His maverick mentality, his unbelievable faith in God, his unwavering courage to charge into the world's hardest (and often most dangerous) places in order to help the most vulnerable people, still drives each and every one of us who are involved in the work he began in 1971."

What follows is the story of Dr. Ward, his love of God, and the subsequent burden for the poor that drove him toward a life of unbelievable courage. It is the biography of a man whom many would later call, "an 'Indiana Jones' of compassion and faith." And as the author and personal friend of Larry's, Norman B. Rohrer, will eloquently remind you in these pages, the stories are often so remarkable that they read like scripts of a Hollywood action movie. If Dr. Ward were still with us, he would most likely chuckle at his good friend's assertion and explain as he had throughout his life, "I am an *ordinary* man, but I serve an *extraordinary* God." You will discover that the effectiveness and necessity of Food for the Hungry's work in today's world are firmly entrenched in the themes of the stories that follow. It is the prayer of the many dedicated men and women who serve in the ranks of Food for the Hungry today, that when you consider the plight of our worlds poor and ask, "*Father, what can I do? I'm just one person,*" you too will be inspired and moved to action by the example of Dr. Larry Ward and his *extraordinary God.*

FOLLOWING are some of the key events in the life of Dr. Larry Ward and Food for the Hungry:

1924	December 14: born in Sidney, New York, youngest of five children and Whitney and Orleva Ward.
1940	July 11: dedicated life to Christian service. Later that same year, licensed to preach – at age fifteen.
1942	High school graduation in Norwich, New York. Honored as "one who has done the most for his school." Entered Wheaton College in September.
1943-46	In military service, doubling as Youth For Christ director in Watertown, South Dakota, while stationed at Army Air Base there. Returned to Wheaton College in September, after brief period of service with Le Tourneau Evangelistic Center in New York.
1947	July 5: married to Lorraine Alice Hustad, RN, in Hibbing, Minnesota.
1949	Graduated "with high honor" from Wheaton College and began full duties with Christian Life magazine.

1949-52	Managing editor of Christian Life. Daughter Sherilyn Sue born June, 1951.
1952-55	Director of Publications, General Association of Regular Baptist Churches and editor of Baptist Bulletin.
1955-56	Director of Educational Services, Gospel Light Publications.
1956-57	First managing editor of Christianity Today.
1957-62	Vice President/Information Services for World Vision; first editor of World Vision Magazine. Began continuous world travels in August 1958—same month in which son Kevin Charles was born (August 6).
1958-65	Executive Secretary of Evangelical Press Association and Director EP News Service
1963-64	Joined Roy Wolfe to form TELL Services as information agency assisting Christian organizations.
1965-70	Rejoined World Vision at urging of his friend and mentor Dr. Bob Pierce, becoming Vice President/Overseas Director. Had major involvement for World Vision in Vietnam (forty-four trips there in forty-eight months).
1969	Awarded Doctor of Humanities degree, Azusa Pacific College, Azusa, CA Conferred Doctor of Laws degree, Yonsei University, Seoul, South Korea
1971	First president of Food for the Hungry International.

1972	One of first evangelical leaders to enter Bangladesh. Met with president, prime minister, and U.N. officials to plan major relief airlift.
1973	Directed earthquake relief in Managua, Nicaragua.
1974	Visited famine areas of Africa's Sahel; expedited assistance to Honduras after Hurricane Fifi. Authored And There Will Be Famines.
1975	April: put first Vietnamese "boat people" in water; led "exodus" of hundreds of refugees from Saigon. Established unique "Hope Village" for 1,100 refugees in Weimar, California.
1976	In Guatemala to meet with disaster relief officials just four weeks before major earthquake and returned immediately to direct massive assistance program. In August, entered war-torn Lebanon on small refugee boat from Cyprus met Dr. Charles Malik (former President, U.N. General Assembly) to initiate relief assistance.
1977	One of first outsiders on the scene after the Romanian earthquake.
1978	Launched "Operation Rescue" mercy ship program for Vietnamese refugee boat people.
1979	First visit to Vietnam since political change.
1980	Began Food for the Hungry refugee assistance programs in Somalia.

1981	Established International Coordination Center for Food for the Hungry International in Geneva, Switzerland. Among three named as 1981 Wheaton College Distinguished Alumni of the Year.
1982	January: with colleague Dr. Tetsunao Yamamori, visited Poland during martial law; began major assistance program there.
1983	Saw longtime dream answered in official formation of Food for the Hungry/Japan in July; completed a major "Disaster Preparation Checklist" for developing countries, presented at disaster relief seminar in Geneva in October.
1984	June 1: in his sixtieth year, resigned as president of Food for the Hungry International, to be succeeded by Dr. Tetsunao Yamamori—completing the full internationalization of the Food for the Hungry program as he had long anticipated.

This is the bare bones outline. After retiring from Food for the Hungry, Larry continued helping people around the world. The above is only the flesh-and-blood substance. The heart of all the above: "This poor man cried, and the Lord heard him."

1
A DIFFERENT WORLD

OVERHEAD a silver jet swept low, its guns chattered as the long tongue of its rocket reached out to strike the earth over and over with violent impacts. From the ground, the smoke of the burning Vietnamese village snaked its dark path upward as far as the eye could see. Standing in the midst of the rubble, a man shook his head bewildered by the tragic scenes of war: from shattered buildings, to frightened children, to the bodies of the dead frozen in grotesque positions- a common result of violent death. His ears rung with the clamor of desperate voices, the sharp and continual crack of small arms fire, the steady thump of mortars.

Slowly the man lifted his face from the hellish scene toward the blue sky overhead. "Father," he prayed aloud, grinding out each word in deep earnestness, "why—*why* have you brought me here? There's so little I can do! *Why?*"

He stood for a moment gazing upward and waiting for an answer. Then, as he slowly lowered his eyes, he noticed something that had been cast on the ground in front of him. As he bent down to pick up the mud-stained and half-burned Bible, his quickening heart beat told him that right there in the dirt and ashes was God's answer to his desperate question.

With a suitcase in one hand and briefcase in the other, he later stood indecisively in the confusion of the Dhaka airport arrival area. Naked children crowded him on all sides as they pleaded and begged for food or money, porters reached insistently for his bags, loud-voiced drivers called to him from nearby bicycle-powered rickshaws hoping for business.

As he looked at his watch, he paused for a quiet moment to ask for help. "Father," his heart cried out in prayer, "I came here to Bangladesh because I thought you were leading me here. But, maybe I should just turn around and go back to Kolkata. I don't know what to do. I don't even know where to start!"

"*Please*, dear God," he prayed desperately, "Show me what to do!"

Just a few short hours later, he found himself sitting in the home of the president of the country of Bangladesh and he prayed again—but this time it was a joyful prayer of thanksgiving: "Thank you, Father, thank you! Now, I at last can see what you want us to do here."

Again, in another country, his eyes lowered as he stood respectfully before His Royal Highness Prince Peter of Greece and Denmark as this royal leader pinned a colorful ribbon on the man's chest. The ornate hotel dining room broke into applause as the Prince concluded his glowing remarks about all this man had done, ". . . for furthering the cause of peace and international understanding."

As the applause continued and guests in the room surged to their feet, the man turned slowly to face them. Stepping to the rostrum, he prayed again. It was an earnest prayer, "O dear God, I want *you* to have all the glory. Please give me the words to say, help me to turn this whole thing upward to you."

The room quieted as he began to speak, "You who know our work, know that everything we do is done in the name of the Lord Jesus Christ and with the desire that people be brought to faith in him. So it is in his name, for him, that I accept this honor—and then lay it at his feet as an act of worship."

Yet again, he found himself sitting on a crude log platform, looking out in wonder at the colorful crowd gathered in the huge thatch-covered temporary auditorium, the man whispered to the missionary friend beside him. "Joe, this is incredible," he marveled. "There must be ten thousand people in here, and thousands more outside. Every tribe in Nagaland must be here, judging from all the different blankets, and just look at the way they are separated into so many language groups for the interpretations."

He broke off the conversation as he heard his name called from the stage. As he walked toward the pulpit, he began to pray. "Father, these people have come with such expectancy. Some of them have walked for days, just to hear your Word. Use me, dear God. I cry out to you. Please. Don't let them be disappointed."

Alone in a quiet room, he pecked away at the small portable typewriter in the center of his desk. Impatiently, he pulled the sheet of typing paper from the machine, wadded it up, and tossed it toward the nearby wastepaper basket. He rolled another sheet of paper into the carriage and was lost in thought. He bent forward with his eyes closed, buried his face in his hands and began to pray, "Dear God, you know how seeing the needs of the people in that war-torn country broke my heart. *Please* help me to write about those desperate needs so clearly now that others will feel it as I did, and want to do something about it."

He sat for a moment before the typewriter considering his words, his head was still bowed in prayer: "O dear God—take me there again, right now. Let me feel it, smell it, ache as I did out there. Help me write it so others will care." As he raised his eyes from prayer, words began to form clearly across the white page, the staccato of the old typewriter hammered away and began to fill the quiet room with hope.

Scenes like the ones sketched in the vignettes above were simply commonplace occurrences in the remarkable life of Larry Ward. For a over quarter of a century, he flew hundreds of thousands of miles each year (about eleven million miles in all); he circled the globe again and again on tireless missions of mercy:

He rode through the winter night on the Chopin Express, the night train from Vienna to Warsaw, and headed into the uncertainties of martial law in Poland.

He stood on the deck of a rescue ship in the South China Sea and scanned the rugged waters with his binoculars looking for that speck in the distance which could be the little Vietnamese fishing boat carrying a frightened band of refugees in their desperate bid for freedom.

He walked through the naked heartbreak of a "famine camp" in northern Kenya and looked down from a tiny plane onto the earthquake-ravaged streets of Managua or Guatemala City in the wake of sudden disaster.

He cried in frustration as he watched a little girl die in Laos because she didn't have enough food to keep her alive and well.

He arrived in prayerful anticipation just beyond the East Appointment Gate in Washington, D.C., readying his mind to enter the White House and advocate for people half a world away that were in desperate need of the basic requirements for life.

No matter the country, the challenge, the heartbreak, Larry Ward would tell you that there was one common factor: he would simply point to the one verse from the Bible he regarded as the central force behind God's profound calling on his own life. In the words of Psalm 34:6, "This poor man cried . . . and the Lord heard him."

Larry Ward was no adventurer, even though some of the chapters of his life (as related in the latter part of this book) might sound like a chapter from a James Bond novel or a CIA history book. If you asked Larry Ward, he would describe himself in these terms: "I am a *very* ordinary guy, with *very* ordinary abilities." He would always conclude with a knowing smile, "But, you know, I serve a *very* extraordinary God."

Larry would explain to his biographer: "If there's one thing about my life which is worth telling, it's the story of the great God who had always been there to listen when I cried out to him in Jesus's name."

His words of longing and prayer became the cornerstone of a mission that has impacted the world for generations. Larry Ward explained the genesis of his mission to the world in simple, straightforward terms, "I guess mine is a different kind of world from that which most people know. But this same wonderful God is available to any other 'poor man' (or woman) willing to ask his help. The greatest experiences of my life have come out of a deep personal sense of inadequacy, when I just had to cry out to him because I needed his help so much."

2

WHAT'S HE REALLY LIKE

A GOOD PLAY needs no epilogue, and the biography of a worthy subject needs no exaggeration to strengthen its appeal. Lawrence Edward Ward would have been the first to acknowledge that everything worth recording about his life was held in what *The Living Bible* describes as "a perishable container" (2 Corinthians 4:7).

He would quite literally agree with the sage Ptahhotep of the twenty-fourth century, B.C., who admonished: "Be cheerful while you are alive." Larry was almost always "up," especially early in the morning. His first wife Lorraine, who passed away before Larry (he was later fortunate enough to find love again and remarried), would always jokingly remark that he was "disgustingly cheerful" or "unfailingly optimistic."

One morning, in a mud hut in Somalia, I recall observing from a nearby bed as Larry got up, stretched, and greeted the day. No one else was awake, but he was already smiling broadly to himself, happy to be in that remote and impoverished refugee camp, full of energy and ready for the day's duties in dust and dirt.

He was blessed with good health, but Larry was not without physical annoyances. A bothersome rash (*lichen planus*) was probably his only outward telltale indication of reaction to deadline and diplomatic pressures through the years—until later in his life, when he passed away from complications of diabetes. Allergies kept his sinuses constantly congested, especially when he was riding in a pressurized airplane cabin, which was the kind of flight that occurred in Larry's work about every third day.

He loved people, but hated gossip of any kind, quitters of any reason, and virtually any form of excuses. A close associate once remarked, "The only time I saw him lose his temper was when someone pronounced a task or project impossible without making what Larry regarded as an honest effort."

As an observer of his work, I would add another: he couldn't stand to see someone slighted, whether it was a timid child in school or a weary passenger being cut out of line by an impatient ticket holder. Once in a German airport when a passenger stepped into line ahead of the people who had been patiently waiting, Larry approached the violator with humor and said, "Excuse me, I'm from *Der Spiegel*. I'm interviewing people who cut into line ahead of others."

Larry held fast to the law of life that he learned from his father: "What you do, do well." When he was concentrating on a task, such as writing an article or a TV script, he had the ability to put the rest of the world aside—and move into a state of focus that almost seemed like a remarkable self-hypnosis. His first wife, Lorraine smiled in tolerant amusement when Larry, pounding away with incredible focus at his typewriter, would call out to her, "Lo, what time is it?" despite the watch on his wrist or the clock on a nearby wall.

Perhaps it is more accurate to say that most of the time she would smile. One day, he apparently stretched that particular string too far. "Lo," he called without looking up, "what does your watch say?"

Lorraine looked at him with a long and icy stare. "Tick tock," she replied finally and firmly. "That's what it says, Larry, 'tick tock!'"

His long time traveling companions, Roy Wolfe and Hal Stack, reported that Larry would completely unpack every time he checked into a hotel or motel, even if just for a short overnight stay. Maybe, they speculated, it was because his hotel room was the only office he knew most of the time.

Larry had a compulsion—an obsession—for neatness. "I suppose I lose a lot of valuable time," he admitted, "because I just have to stop and reorganize—my desk top, my papers, my room—at intervals of the day and night."

In the fall of 1982, Larry enrolled for a special four-week course at Duke University Medical School involving medical, nutritional, and psychological components. He was anxious to get competent help with his own weight control and dietary problems, particularly with the unusual (if not unique) complexities posed by his travel schedule, which took him away 90 percent of the time. He found the psychological and behavioral aspects stimulating, felt that the nutritional studies were most valuable for his work as well as for his personal life, and was encouraged by the very thorough medical examinations he received showing heart, lungs, and vital organs exceptionally healthy for a man of fifty-seven.

On his travels, Larry would constantly forget his glasses (especially sunglasses). There was a scattering of them all over the world in airplane seat pockets, restaurant tables, hotel checkout counters, and rental cars. His obsession about time related to a larger principle in Larry's life. I often heard him pray in the morning something like this: "Lord, we thank you for this day. As men measure time, here's a day we have never lived before in eternity, a day we shall never live again. Please put into it by your grace what you want it to include. Help us today to invest this gift of time wisely, to live this day the way we will wish we had lived it when we meet you face to face." Perhaps that's why Larry was up and working by four o'clock most mornings—and often times much earlier. He seemed to need less sleep than most people and could catnap in automobiles, trains, planes, or buses at any time he wished.

The last message Larry received from his own mother focused on this element of precious time. Orleva Ward died on Christmas Day, 1957. "How terrible," said a sympathetic nurse, "to die on Christmas." Larry smiled through his tears and replied: "Our mother would have said, 'How wonderful to meet my Lord on the day men celebrate as his birthday.'"

Larry used to recall how he and his dad, brothers, and sisters, maintained a constant twenty-four-hour vigil at her bedside, talking to her and trying to coax her out of the coma into which she had suddenly slipped on his birthday, December 14. He explained, "We prayed that she would open her eyes for just a moment and at least say *something* to us—some last word before she died. But she never woke up until she woke up in heaven. She never spoke until she lifted her voice in praise to God up there."

After the funeral, Larry came home to find a stack of sympathy cards mixed up with the Christmas greetings, which had arrived in his absence. But in the pile was a different kind of card and he was puzzled for a moment until he realized it was a birthday card. He had forgotten all about his own birthday during those long and trying days in the hospital. When he opened a card with familiar handwriting to check the signature, he explained, "My heart gave a kind of leap that I know you will understand. It was from my mother. Apparently the card was on its way to me while I was rushing to be with her. It must have been written just before she went into the coma. There was just a brief comment about the busyness of the pre-Christmas season, and then Mother added, 'This week, I must make the time count.'"

Larry seemed to italicize those words in his own life: *This week, I must make the time count.* "What a way," he said, "to begin one's last week of conscious life on earth. What a wonderful way to begin every week, every day."

The pressure of time led Larry to prepare detailed time-phased worksheets for each day of his life. These schedules probably led him to take on more than he should have, to try very often to fill the slots with more work than was humanly possible. Still, Larry's output of work was prodigious. Donald Simonsen, a member of both the U.S. and International boards of Food for the Hungry, recalled how Larry returned from a trip to Israel, spent one day at home in office conferences, and then promptly departed on a trip to Asia. "During that one busy day at home," said Don, "despite jet lag and all, Larry wrote over twenty letters to the different government officials he had just contacted in Israel. He sent me copies, and each one of the letters was different and personal."

Larry carried a small tape recorder at all times, and dictated wherever he was—even while driving down a busy freeway in the States or speeding along an *autobahn* in Europe. He shaved it close at airports, often arriving barely in time to board his plane. This practice changed with age, but on so many occasions you could observe Larry squeaking into the airplane cabin just as the door was closing.

On one occasion, Gene and Loretta Furlong drove him to Los Angeles International Airport and arrived at the check-in counter to find his plane had just left. They could see it taxiing down the runway toward takeoff position. The Furlongs saw Larry whisper something to an attendant, then start running—baggage in hand, coat and tie flying in the wind. The plane returned to the tarmac, and Larry clambered up the ramp. He waved once, and then was swallowed by the jet that would take him half a world away.

Lorraine and Larry Ward always maintained a deep love for the children of the world and a very special love for their own son and daughter. "It's wonderful watching the children grow up," Lorraine once observed, "but a special delight when your own children become your adult friends. In fact, Larry and I regard our Sheri and her Bill, and our Kevin and his Penni, as our closest friends. We spend our holidays together, take trips with them when we can, and get together for dinner whenever possible."

"And how we thank God," she added, "when we see them all active in church. Larry was gone so much of the time when they were growing up. We have seen other families, which have paid a terrible price in misunderstanding and separation and spiritual bitterness. But God somehow gave Sheri and Kevin a sense of shared purpose in their daddy's work, even when they were very small."

To Larry that "somehow" was easily once explained: "Lorraine accepted it as perhaps no one else could—or would. But perhaps 'accepted' is not exactly the right word. She led the kids in a very positive participation in the work. She didn't merely 'accept' it—she made it her ministry. Not that it ever was easy. I think, in fact, that it has gotten more difficult all through the years. But she turned a potential tragedy into a triumph."

If you had lots of extra time to spend, you would have loved to hear Larry and Lorraine talk about their grandchildren: Melissa Lorraine (Moy) and Courtnie Brooke (Ward). "I used to think I was the 'fastest draw in the West' when it came to pulling out their pictures," admitted Larry, "but somehow Lorraine always had hers out while I was still reaching. She belongs in the *Guinness Book of World Records*. By the way—have you seen our latest pictures?"

Sometimes when Larry looked into the face of a starving child in some Third World famine or refugee situation, he felt that for a moment he saw his own grandchildren, Melissa or Courtnie. He often would tell the story about a little girl in Laos, dying before his eyes, who turned out to be almost exactly the same age as his beloved Sheri. He regarded that as one of the specific incidents that led to the founding of Food for the Hungry.

Tears always filled his eyes when he related an incident involving two-year-old Melissa. She was sitting in her high chair with her cereal bowl untouched. Her spoon was motionless in the air; her little lower lip was protruding.

"Melissa," exclaimed her mother, Sheri, "what's wrong?"

Looking straight ahead, little Melissa quavered: "Some kids, no food."

To really know Larry Ward, you had to watch him around a bunch of kids. I recall an incident on the mainland of China at the Sun Yat Sen School where we stopped for a short visit. Larry and I picked up Ping-Pong paddles for a quick game on the compound of People's Republic of China's prized school. Soon the youngsters were squealing with delight at the antics of this big American. He performed deliberate stumbles, clever backhand shots, wild serves, and even pretended to panic. It sent up cheers of laughter from the playground and balconies circling the arena.

High up in the mountains of Taiwan, Larry taught the Chinese-speaking kids to chant, "Hoo-ray for the Dodgers." All around the world, he taught that chant to children who may be using it even today without knowing they are rooting for a faraway Los Angeles baseball team. Anthropologists and ethnologists of future generations may have a tough time trying to figure out the origin of his chant!

Dulal Borpujari tells of a heartwarming scene in Phnom Penh, Cambodia, shortly after that country opened to the outside world. "Larry got one little child to imitate him, then another, and finally many others joined in. They would run when he did, stop when he stopped, and cheer for the Dodgers when he signaled—all the time laughing their heads off. It was beautiful, but it was also deeply moving. I saw parents watching—laughing and crying at the same time. Some of them had probably never heard their children laugh before—certainly not like this. Soon about three hundred of them were following their American 'Pied Piper' down the street—until a stern-faced guard with a gun chased them away."

In the early 1980s, Karen Burton Mains dedicated her beautifully written book *The Fragile Curtain* (a compassionate look at the world of refugees) "to Larry and Lorraine Ward, and to others like them, who have seen the world in torment thousands of times and are still moved to tears." Mains's words were a fitting description, for to travel with Larry through what he referred to as "the world of hunger" was to sense again and again the depths of his genuine compassion. Dr. W. S. Mooneyham once introduced Larry as having "a computer for a brain, a marshmallow for a heart."

At the time, twenty-eight people died of hunger or related causes every minute (most of them children). When Larry reminded us of that, you knew exactly how he felt. When he quoted the statistic that each day 40,000 people died just because they didn't have food enough to keep them alive and well, he almost always would quickly add: "They die one at a time, so we can help them one at a time. *But each one is one too many.*"

The teenaged Larry Ward who dived unhesitatingly through the window of a runaway car to save a little boy's life was the same Larry Ward who drove himself on a constant mission of mercy through the battlefields and disaster zones and famine areas of the earth for much of his own life.

So what drove him? Larry would honestly answer that question with a simple phrase: "The love of Christ constrains me."

When he discussed the world he was able to experience, tears would well up in his eyes. It didn't matter whether it was a personal conversation; he was speaking in a church service; or he was reporting on TV or radio. Larry always made a clear distinction between emotion and compassion. He often quoted the late Bob Pierce: "Pity is something you feel. Compassion is something you do."

Theologically, Larry firmly held to typical Baptist convictions. He would also quietly testify to the impact of the Holy Spirit on his own life. He once explained, "On my first trip to Bangladesh in 1972, I was a guest in the home of Cal and Marion Olsen—missionaries of the Assemblies of God and two of the most Christ-like people I know. In my room, I found several books on various Pentecostal subjects, such as 'the Baptism of the Holy Spirit.' Frankly, I wasn't too impressed, even though I was trying to read with an open mind. One book was by a Baptist pastor relating his experience of 'speaking in tongues,' but I felt the scholarship was dubious."

Larry continued, "I closed the books and knelt to pray before going to sleep. And as I did, there suddenly flashed into my mind the words A. B. Simpson regarding the 'gifts' of the Holy Spirit. As I recalled it, he said something like 'Seek not, shun not.' No sooner had I remembered those words than I suddenly *felt* the presence of the Holy Spirit, as I had never experienced him before. Welling up within me were great surges of the soul, great paeans of praise, overwhelming feelings of worship, beyond anything I could express in words of my own. All I could do was to trust the Holy Spirit himself—'Who makes intercession for us with groanings which cannot be uttered'—to carry these deep feelings to the Father for me in the form of articulated prayer."

On another occasion, while Larry was in Arizona, he responded to an urgent call from a friend with a great spiritual need. He rushed to a plane and flew to Sacramento to meet with her and her brother. After a brief period of conversation with them, Larry looked at her and said quietly, "Are you trying to tell me that you feel you are under demonic influence or pressure?" When she nodded tearful assent, Larry instantly dropped to his knees to pray. He recounted, "What happened next is too sacred to describe, except to say that God himself was suddenly in that room, and the Holy Spirit took over in prayer. "When I (we?) finished praying, there was warmth—a glow, an indescribable peace—which filled the room. All three of us felt it. None of us had to comment on it. We just knelt there and smiled at each other, in gentle and perfect understanding."

Illustrations of Larry Ward's compassion could fill several books. Compassion was the driving force through his entire life and ministry. In 1958, Larry visited Taiwan's Lo Sheng Sanatorium for people afflicted with Hansen's disease (also known as leprosy), with his missionary friend Lillian Dickson. In what Lil Dickson called the "Ward Nearest Heaven," Larry found a man with "a radiant testimony" for the Lord Jesus Christ. The man showed all the signs of his disease. His skin had the leathery texture; his hands were just stumps. He was blind. But the light of the gospel had reached that dark corner, and the man wanted everyone to know it. His testimony was simple. Whenever he sensed that someone had entered that room, he raised his right hand toward heaven.

Larry's description of that first encounter was memorable, "I knew what the upraised hand was saying. It said, 'Here's where my faith is based. Here's where my hope is placed.' It was his way of pointing us toward God, of inclining our thoughts toward the Savior. This man wasn't doing much, by usual human standards. But he was doing all he could with what little he had. God helped us to do the same."

The story has a beautiful sequel. About a year later, Larry had returned to Lo Sheng Sanatorium, back in the Ward Nearest Heaven. He stood again by the bedside of this man who months before had made such a deep impression on him. But now there was a difference. The man's breathing was labored, and his strength seemed almost gone.

"Look, Larry," said Lil Dickson. "He's so weak. He can't even raise his hand anymore."

But then both Lil and Larry noticed something. They looked at each other in tearful wonder as they watched the man's right hand—and saw what was left of his little finger twitch and move against the white sheet. "Why—he's trying to raise his hand again," Lil explained, "but all he can do is move that little finger."

Larry and Lillian Dickson prayed for the man, and then started on to continue their rounds through the hospital. But Larry couldn't leave the room until he went over to stand by the bed once more. And once again he saw that little finger struggle to move. Larry Ward's heart told him what to do. He reached down, carefully took that wasted hand in his own, and then—supporting the arm—gently lifted it up . . . until he saw a smile flicker across that tired face, as once more a child of God could praise his Creator with an upraised hand.

My wife Virginia and I stood with Larry in the teeming cities of Asia, in the forgotten corners of famine in Africa, in refugee centers around the world. We can bear witness that when Larry Ward saw the multitudes, he had compassion on them.

We watched as "this poor man cried" to the Lord.

And we were there when he just plain cried.

3

"FACT, FAITH, FEELING . . ."

TO LARRY WARD, God himself was the fundamental fact of the universe. Larry was fond of quoting "fact, faith, feeling" as the divine order for—well, just about everything.

"Our eternal salvation is based upon the fact of God himself," Larry maintained. "*He* exists, *He* loves, *He* gave his Son to die in our place. *He* calls us to himself—and *He* gives us faith to respond.

"If someone tells me he has sincerely trusted Christ to be his Savior, in obedience to the Word of God, but somehow doesn't 'feel' saved, I tell him not to worry about it. The 'feeling' will come, as the Holy Spirit works in his life and as he grows spiritually. But we start with the *fact* of a loving God who invites us to come to Him, and promises that He will not 'cast us out' when we do."

Similarly, with reference to his work for the hungry, Larry would tell people that even though they may not have seen the world of hunger as he had seen it, and even though they may not "feel" its heartbreak as he felt it (maybe because that hadn't seen it firsthand, or perhaps because their emotional makeup was not the same), there was still no excuse for them not to get helpfully involved. "Again," he would say, "we start with the face of God. He cares about the hungry. We know He does, because there is more than abundant evidence of this in His Word. And he has specifically mandated us to do something about it. We find that over and over again, in the Bible."

"HOLY BIBLE, BOOK DIVINE . . ."

Larry Ward didn't seem to care much about "things." Cars, clothing, material possessions in general just didn't "interest him," *unless* they somehow related to helping other people.

But there was one thing Larry always treasured: his Bible. Someone once observed, "Larry doesn't hold his Bible, he caresses it."

While Larry Ward himself would always warn against "bibliolatry" (worship of the Word instead of the God for whom it speaks), he admitted to a constant feeling of "reverential awe" when he handled and read the Bible. Larry would never put anything (such as another book) on top of his Bible. If someone else did, he would quickly remove it.

I once saw him with tears in his eyes as he stood behind a church pulpit and addressed himself to the book in his hand (quoting and old hymn): "Holy Bible, book divine—precious treasure, thou art *mine*!"

No doubt many people contributed to this attitude. Larry himself would cite observing his own father, "He fell in love with the Bible almost the moment he became a Christian." And his father-in-law Rev. L. P. Hustad, who Larry explained was, "a big 'man's man' who would weep as he preached, just from the sheer joy of being privileged to communicate the truth of God." He pointed to the example of faithful preacher friends such as R. T. Ketcham, A. W. Tozer, and the biblically-oriented ministries of former pastors such as Reginald Matthews, John Anderson, Bernard Travaille, and Guy Davidson. In Wheaton College's 1946 fall evangelistic series (Larry's first years back after military service), Dr. Merv Rosell left a lasting impression on Larry's life. The two remained lifelong close friends. Larry was fond of describing Merv with Cliff Barrows's phrase, "The Apostle of Encouragement."

No matter where he was or how early the hour, Larry's first appointment each day was always with God—with the Bible (usually a chapter each day) and his *Living Light* daily reading.

"THE WAY, THE TRUTH . . ."

Larry's love for God's truth carried over into a firm stand for truth and honesty in every area of life.

"My dear mom," he recalled with a chuckle, "knew how to stop me in my tracks if I started to come up with a little boy lie. She would just look into my eyes and ask me, 'Honest?' That may not have been very grammatical, but it was very effective. No way could I lie to her! I would just sorta melt and say something like, 'No, Mom. It wasn't a tiger; it was just a big ole cat. Well, not such a big one, I guess. And he didn't really chase me; he just looked at me kinda mean like...'"

This preoccupation with truth was only intensified through Larry's editorial background. To him, words were almost sacred. He felt that they were a gift of God, made for full and honest communication.

Larry explained, "I try to be an appreciative listener in church. I have to give out so much that I am always grateful when I can take in. But I admit it really bothers me when I hear some preacher tell a more-than-twice-told-tale as his own, or bend a story or adapt the punch-line so it neatly fits his own sermon outline."

And perhaps this is why he regarded gossip as such a serious sin, "I knew a preacher once," he would explain, "whose ministry was almost ruined by careless talk. Later it was found that none of it was true."

One of Larry's colleagues once suffered a painful marriage breakup and subsequently remarried. Larry spent months in a counseling role, along with a professional counselor. He was acquainted with every detail of the situation. It was painful for him, for he loved both the people involved. But the greatest pain came when another not that close to the divorce began to pick it up and broadcast it to the world—without care or appreciation for the facts.

Larry would shake his head while recalling: "One particular 'Christian leader'—who had no firsthand contact with the divorce—was quoted to me by people in various parts of the country (and of the world, for that matter) as having brought this up to them and being very critical of my colleague. But when I confronted him (honestly wondering if he might somehow have information I myself had missed), he denied even having made those statements, which other people were independently attributing to him. Very strange! And then an organization that had given us some money told us it had been strongly criticized by a 'Christian leader' for doing so because of this same situation—and once again the same inaccurate statements had been made. I guess it's true, sadly true, that a lie can go around the world while truth is still on the launching pad."

The significant thing about this instance was that Larry wasn't just being loyal to an old friend. He was standing for the truth as he saw it.

THE CHURCH HIS BODY

Another concept very important to Larry Ward was that of the Church (all true believers in Christ around the world) as the mystical "body" of Christ. To be sure, Larry (probably because of his Baptist background) was very much a local church enthusiast. He believed in "the church on the corner as well as the church in the world. But he always felt a special and strong commitment to that "body" of believers around the world. And this was reflected even in the basic organization of Food for the Hungry.

During our days together at World Vision, I often heard Larry sketch his view of the ideal organizational pattern for any worldwide mission type organization: a truly international staff; operating from a neutral base (such as Geneva, Switzerland) with "support entities" in those countries which could supply both funding and human resources. He deeply appreciated World Vision's commitment to effective internationalization and was an active member of their committee designed to bring it about.

When Food for the Hungry was formed in 1971, this was his chance to build from the ground up another agency with true international character. Today it exists as an international coordination center; network of service offices scattered throughout the world in places of desperate need; a truly international staff, with many different nationalities, director-level and up; and support entities in various parts of the world, with more "on the drawing board."

The entity in Japan was of particular interest to Larry. He would explain his involvements with Bob Pierce in the Osaka and

Tokyo crusades in 1959 and 1961, and was very grateful to Bob for the concept of organizations as "the servant of the Church" around the world. He was deeply grateful to friends such as missionary Joe Gooden in Japan for reinforcing that understanding.

It was during the Osaka crusade in 1959 that Larry actually put down in specifics the organizational concepts that were to find eventual and specific reality in Food for the Hungry. It was a source of great satisfaction to him, therefore, in 1981 to sit in Osaka with a founding group of Japanese Christians as they organized Japan International Food for the Hungry.

The concept was not that of Japan's being a recipient country—one being helped—but rather on supplying "food and funds and friends" to the rest of the world. Larry explained: "I have marveled at the way Japanese ingenuity, technology and managerial genius have impacted the world. I have coveted that same influence on behalf of the work of God in the world, and specifically for the hungry."

LOOKING AHEAD . . .

And it was probably a commitment to all of these things—truth, honesty, and the worldwide family of God—which led Larry to a very important decision in 1981.

He had always been very candid about his role in Food for the Hungry. "I didn't have to be the head of anything," he would say. "There was just a job to be done; I saw no one else doing it with an organization specifically designed to help the hungry as its prime objective, really 'the only string on its guitar,' and so with a group of concerned friends, I launched Food for the Hungry."

Larry was keenly aware of a pattern he had seen very often in Christian work. He had served on many boards, and had been in close touch with a great variety of Christian organizations. He had often watched an organization begin with an entrepreneurial founder—and in time outgrow its founder.

Larry chuckled as he described this sort of scenario, "The day comes when the organization has outgrown its founder. The specialists have arrived—and now that generalist-founder is the bottleneck. So everyone wonders what to do. They shake their heads, look over at the founder in the corner and whisper something like, 'Poor 'ole Larry. How are we going to tell him? It will break his heart.'"

Whether or not Food for the Hungry was at that point or even beginning to approach it in the early 1980s didn't matter. Larry's commitment to the hungry was such that he was more than willing to step aside for the good of the organization. He startled his board in July 1981, with the bold recommendation that one of his chief colleagues, Japanese-born Dr. Tetsunao Yamamori, be named President Elect of the organization.

He proposed at least a two-year transition period, to assist Dr. Yamamori in taking over the complex aspects of both the international program and the support aspect, as well as to also acquaint both government leadership worldwide and the support constituencies (in the United States, primarily) with Dr. Yamamori.

Larry explained, "Ted Yamamori had a deep devotion to Christ, a strong and effective leadership style—and a managerial genius. Food for the Hungry has arrived at a place where it needs this kind of leadership, and I know that Dr. Yamamori will take the organization far beyond any heights that it could ever reach under my leadership alone."

Larry Ward and his successor, Dr. Yamamori, were very different personalities. But they had developed a close bond of fellowship in helping the hungry and maintained a very effective working relationship based on their strong mutual respect. Larry agreed to serve for a time as board chairman, after Dr. Yamamori assumed the presidency of Food for the Hungry in 1984. He was particularly happy about Dr. Yamamori's experience, as a disciple of Dr. Donald McGavran, in the field of church growth. To Larry, the way to do relief and development so they actually result in evangelism and in the growth of the church around the world was to maintain strong ties to the national churches—to work in effective partnership with them.

That was always Dr. Yamomori's conviction and working pattern, and was one of the reasons why Larry Ward would say of Dr. Yamorori, "I thank God for him so very much." Larry viewed Dr. Yamamori as a strong "team leader"—and knew he would be ably assisted by Vice President Bill Moy in the U.S., and by Vice

Presidents Homer Dowdy, Dulal Borpujari, and John Fitzstevens on the international side.

What was ahead for Larry Ward, as he stepped away from the active presidency of Food for the Hungry? "I don't know, exactly," Larry would say, "but I am very much at peace. I do want to keep on being 'a voice to plead the cause of the poor and needy,' and I expect to be much more involved in speaking ministries throughout the United States and in Canada—and around the world. I have all sorts of notes tucked away here and there as the bases for articles and books I want to write. So we will just see how God leads, step by step."

One thing was certain. Larry meant it when he said it back there on the shores of Canandaigua Lake at Le Tourneau Christian Camp in 1940: "Where He leads me, I will follow."

Just how deep was Larry Ward's commitment to truth and "rightness"? There's a rather clear indication in a signed and notarized statement he issued in August 1981. It was officially witnessed by Lorraine, on behalf of the family, and by Tetsunao Yamamori, representing Food for the Hungry. Larry had been deeply concerned about the rise of international terrorism and the spectacle of Americans abroad being held for ransom. His statement directed that in the event of his being kidnapped or held hostage "no negotiations of any kind are to be conducted with terrorist groups."

Although a household name in the US he was not, Larry was constantly in the world's hot spots. He had been a dinner guest in presidential palaces in such areas as Bangladesh, Vietnam, Nicaragua, and Guatemala. He had official meetings with controversial leaders such as Nicaragua's Anastasio Somoza and Bangladesh's Sheik Mujibur Rahman—both of whom were later assassinated. He had escaped coups and near-coups in Thailand and Bolivia, and had been with some of Lebanon's top leaders in the midst of their shooting war.

Aware that, humanly speaking, he just "might be in the right place at the wrong time" and be captured, Larry stated: "It is my specific desire that not one cent of money or moment of time be expended in any negotiations for my release. "He summed it up in a time when terrorism was new to the world: "I fully support the present strong position taken against terrorism by the U.S.

government. International 'gangsterism' must be stopped. As a relief worker, I am totally expendable. As a Christian, I gladly put myself in the hand of our all-powerful God."

Larry suggested that if he was kidnapped or held hostage, his notarized letter should simply be published with this notation for captors: "He's all yours. You can have him."

4

SACRED JOYS OF HOME

NOTABLE PERSONS usually enter this world incognito. Ralph Waldo Emerson liked to put his hand reverently upon the head of any child, thinking he "may be patting the head of a future president."

On December 14, 1924, in Sidney, New York, Max, June, Whitney, and Doris patted the head of their little brother to whom their parents gave the name Lawrence Edward.

A.W. Tozer pointed out that if you get a good mother it will not do to be too particular about your father: "You cannot have both." This boy, however, seemed to have had both. From thin, wiry, gregarious, artistic Whitney Ward, Larry inherited a fondness for people; his chunky little mother, Orleva, gave him a rugged physical constitution, a warm and optimistic spirit, and a calm disposition, which left him unflappable in the most unnerving of situations.

A person passing by the Ward house in upstate New York during the Roaring Twenties might have seen Whitney dancing for his children as he had done with the Hi Henry Minstrels, or juggling Orleva's best china, or entertaining them with his ventriloquist dummy perched on his knee. A passerby during the Christmas season of 1926 would have seen something quite different: Orleva hurrying with cold packs to cool the fevered brow of her youngest boy. Or

Whitney sitting beside the crib watching pneumonia attempt to steal the life of his son. When doctors could do no more, Whitney stood awkwardly beside the crib and lifted his eyes. Strange recollections of forgotten convictions stirred within. "God," he whispered, "if you'll heal my son, he's yours."

Before the sun rose, Larry began to recover. The encounter had driven a stake for righteousness into the soul of Whitney Ward that God would later claim, partly through the witness of that youngest Ward boy for whom the father had prayed.

When economic challenges touched Larry's father, he moved the family into his mother's big brick house in Cooperstown, New York. Larry's grandmother's house was a suitable playground for the imaginative children who roamed from attic to basement to the barn out back, and who seldom found the cookie jar on the cellar steps empty.

Sitting high up on a hayloft one day, Larry called out to his siblings, "Watch me fly!" The preschooler leaped straight to the barn floor, bruised but unbroken. On another day during a game in the barn, Larry fell through an open door and was propelled out above the barnyard. His brothers and sisters rushed down the stairs expecting to see him torn and bleeding from such a long unexpected fall, maybe even dead. But the only injury was the absence of breath that dramatic gasping and some crying quickly restored.

"The spankings we four older kids received for 'not watching Larry' hurt us more than his bruises hurt him," recalled his sister June as she recounted the day Larry rode his tricycle down a flight of stairs with a paring knife in his hand.

The world of 1928 was relatively small for the youngest Ward. He knew little beyond the appointed rounds of his tricycle and the warm protection of Grandma Hine's lap, where he learned to read. As a boy of four, he caught on to sight-reading, not just words, but also whole sentences and eventually paragraphs. The earliest book he remembers reading was Sir Walter Scott's classic *Ivanhoe*, recounting of the return of King Richard the Lionhearted from captivity. Grandma Hine's early training helped him to eventually read by pages rather than word by word. Before he had finished elementary school, Larry could read 930 words per minute with almost total comprehension. This ability would later give him an edge in his editorial and writing endeavors.

In addition to loving books, Larry Ward also maintained a deep passion for sports. One day at Main Street Elementary School in Norwich, he ran through virtually the entire school in a football scrimmage, reaching the goal line with this necktie torn off and his shirt shredded. He eagerly accepted a pair of boxing gloves to fight in the selected fraternity of pintsized sportsmen at East Main School by knocking down Clif Frink with one punch, a kid so agile he later became an AAU boxer. To Larry, it was all fun. "I wasn't mad at anybody," he told his mother after the boxing victory.

As a seventh grader in Norwich Junior High, he hit four home runs in five times at bat in a softball game—the first in the district's newly organized 1936 sports program. A local newspaper, *The Norwich Evening Sun*, headlined his achievement: "Ward Hits Four Homers."

Before the Norwich Municipal Pool was built, swimming required a hike up to the railroad bridge north of town. Larry and his friends would swing out on a rope, Tarzan style, to plunge into the creek. Sometimes they would stand on the train tracks as the Delaware and Lackawana engine approached and jump only at the last possible moment, the train's horn blaring and its brakes hissing.

In the late weeks of 1934's winter, when the wooded hills of Norwich showed signs of spring, the Ward family all were unknowingly headed for a big change. Larry's classmate, Levi Brooker, invited him to tag along one afternoon at two thirty to what was called an "early release" class at Calvary Baptist Church, which would allow them to get out of school early.

"It's not like school," his friend Levi explained, "It's fun."

The idea of church was not appealing, but an early afternoon release from school was too good to pass up. Larry persuaded his sisters June and Doris and brother Whitney to go with him to the Regular Baptist Church on Birdsall Street. Evangelist Adam Lutzweiler was ready. The versatile visiting minister entertained the children with his marimba and told them a simple story from the Bible. He shared with them the claims of Jesus Christ and invited them to say yes to the Savior's call.

Whitney and Orleva were amazed by what they heard coming out of the mouths of their babies. Somewhere in the past the father had faced these claims and turned away. Orleva had been a Methodist, but had lapsed because of her husband's lack of interest. Now on Easter Sunday 1934, they found themselves seated in Calvary Baptist Church watching as four of their children were baptized. The youthful testimonies were heard; and then the children were lowered into the baptismal waters where they were identified with Christ in his death, burial, and resurrection.

Pastor Norman MacPherson delivered a short message that evening. He finished by inviting sinners in the audience to make their peace with God. Larry's father, Whitney Earl Ward, was the first one in the aisle. He practically ran to the altar with Orleva right behind him. It was quite an Easter celebration with hugs, warm words of praise to God, resolution, and joy.

Larry had a different father from that night on. Whitney fell instantly in love with the Scriptures. It was not unusual for Larry to come home after midnight from a wrestling match to find his father at the kitchen table poring over the Bible with *Bancroft's Systematic Theology* at his side. He itinerated as a lay preacher throughout the area, gave his testimony at every opportunity, painted Scripture verses on his car, and preached on street corners.

In gratitude to Calvary Baptist Church for his regeneration, he painted a life-size portrait of Christ over the baptistery. Whitney joined The Gideons and helped to distribute copies of the Bible throughout upstate New York. God had remembered Whitney's prayer beside the "dying bed" of his baby son and had responded by bringing light and life and salvation to his entire house.

5

GOAL TO GO

LARRY WAS THIRTEEN in 1938 when he lined up with incoming freshmen at Norwich High. Four years later, he graduated with high honors and had earned the coveted George McMullen Award "for doing the most for his school." He had also distinguished himself as the winner of more awards and honors than anyone else to that date at Norwich High.

His school buddy David Miller remembers Larry as "always the center of attentions at school. Girls, boys, and teachers liked him. He seldom took a book home to study, but managed to earn the top grades. Larry won letters in football, wrestling, and track. He was also active in various organizations and was often the president of groups ranging from the Chi Alpha Honor Society to the Boys' Athletic Council."

With his friend David, Larry hitchhiked to football games on the Ivy League circuit, attended the popular Boys' State forum in Syracuse, and seemed to have no more important goal than to please his Coach, Kurt Beyer, at Norwich High.

"When the various teams would travel to out-of-town events," David recalled, "everyone wanted to be in the same car as Larry. He was an endless reservoir of humorous stories and puns. One time, only the best players on our football team went to a game on Long

Island. Larry went, but on his return, he noted my crestfallen state because I had not been chosen.

"'Aw, you didn't miss anything,' he told me. 'I'm sorry I went.' He proceeded to tell me that the team lost, that he was sick on the bus, and that the entire trip was one I should be happy indeed to have missed—all this just to make me feel better. He was compassionate even then."

The trait of fighting for the underdog emerged in high school. In front of Larry in one of his classes sat a mild little Church of the Nazarene kid, the shy Howard Newton. "The teacher that year was probably an alcoholic," Larry said, recalling the experiences. "She would drag into class each morning with an enormous hangover. Nobody in the class knew what was wrong with her."

She asked Howard a question one morning, which he misunderstood. The teacher angrily scolded him with bitter words and humiliated him in front of the entire class. Larry jumped to his feet. "That's it!" he shouted. "I've had it!"

Wow, he thought, *what do I do now?*

The teacher leveled a finger at him. "You're a Communist!" she shouted back. "You're a Communist agitator and you're up to no good. Go to the principal's office immediately."

Trembling as he walked out of the room, Larry glumly made his way to the office of Russell L. Hogue. Teachers had always been his friends. So had the principal. Now he had blown it. "I just felt sorry for Howie Newton," Larry would explain. "He was innocent and I couldn't help myself."

"Well, Larry," the principal replied, "Your teacher has a problem. We all know about it. Probably it would be best to have you switch classes."

Coach Kurt Beyer, who later earned a place in the National Interscholastic Hall of Fame, became an idol to the youngest Ward at Norwich High. Coach could coax heroic efforts from his boys on the playing fields. When Stanford University made the T-formation famous on the football field, Coach Beyer was the first in New York to bring it into high school football, and Larry Ward was one of the first T-formation quarterbacks. Coach Beyer drilled his teams in the fundamentals. He was clever enough to know the limitation and the strong points of each team.

In 1937, Leo Bolley from Syracuse came on the radio to announce his selections for the all-state football team.

"This year my job is easy," Bolley began. One by one he named the players of the undefeated *and* unscored-on Norwich High School team, including Larry.

At the height of his football career as a high school sophomore, Larry broke his right leg in a game. As a senior, he broke the left one. For weeks, he hobbled on his appointed campus rounds with crutches—his brothers and sisters proud of their little brother who had "given his all" for dear old Norwich High.

Larry wanted badly to play basketball, but at five feet, six inches tall, his height made it a challenge. Wrestling offered a new contest of individual strength and skill. Since Coach needed another man on the wrestling team, Larry decided that would be his winter sport. The evening of Larry's first match took him to Van Hornesville High School. His opponent had hair all over his chest and the skill and strength expected to go with it. In a few seconds, Larry was pinned. Humiliated, he shook hands and headed for the shower. Basketball looked more and more appealing. But the more he thought about wrestling, the more he was challenged by it. He would stick around until he won some matches to erase the memory of this first embarrassing defeat. Besides, if being on the wrestling team was what Coach wanted, Larry would do it.

Endless exercises for his neck muscles pushed his shirt size up. His already broad shoulders grew thick, and his grip became like iron. In one of his last high school wrestling matches, he went back to Van Hornesville and wrestled the brother of the guy who had pinned him at the start. Larry took him down in thirty seconds.

"Wrestling teaches independence," he would say. "In football, you could miss a catch or fumble the ball and the team would still be there. But in wrestling, it's you out there alone against your opponent, and that teaches a special kind of personal responsibility."

Will Rogers said he never met a man he didn't like. Larry could probably say that too, but he could also say quite confidently, "I've never met a man I couldn't beat."

Larry penned the senior class' motto at Norwich: "He profits most who serves best." He also wrote the class poem which showed his knowledge of a world beyond the confines of upstate New York, a world then plunged into global war, a world in need which could offer a place for him to serve:

A world of turmoil,
A world of strife,
We see as we stand
On the threshold of life . . .
But we face a bright tomorrow.

All history has been
A record of war.
We look to the future,
Expecting more . . .
Yet we face a bright tomorrow.

Our future is bright because
We carry light and truth
and liberty
To a world of darkness.

His passion for sports directed his goal toward a career in coaching until that memorable night of July 11, 1940. As a staff worker at LeTourneau Camp on Lake Canandaigua, New York, he was in the tabernacle that summer night when Ralph W. Neighbour got up to preach. His delivery was unpretentious, his message now forgotten. But the urgency of his appeal became the voice of God to the young staffer, Larry Ward.

As the youthful audience sang softly, "Where He leads me I will follow," Larry decided, "That's for me." He walked forward, stood in sawdust at the rustic altar, and tearfully gave to the Lord the reins of his heart. At the age of fifteen Larry was licensed to preach by Calvary Baptist Church of Norwich.

6

INTO THE BRAZEN THROAT OF WAR

THE WINDS OF WAR were blowing briskly that spring day of 1942 when Larry was called into the office of Principal Russell L. Hogue at Norwich High. Graduation was a few weeks away. Selected members of the faculty had gathered, and Larry was asked to take a seat.

"Well!" Principal Hogue exclaimed, rubbing his hands together. "Larry, we have some good news for you today."

The faculty members beamed.

Mr. Hogue picked up a sheaf of papers, tapped them on his desk to make them even, and then handed them to his star pupil. "We have here a full scholarship to Duke University in Durham, North Carolina, for Lawrence Edward Ward."

"There's a theology school there, too," added Guidance Director Marcia Stewart enthusiastically, knowing of Larry's Christian commitment. "You could go right into that, with full tuition, after you finish university."

Larry hesitated. He could read on their faces what his response should have been.

"Thanks," he said, promising to read material carefully.

He had noticed earlier an obscure news items on the sports page of *Binghamton Sun* that the wrestling team of Wheaton College in Illinois had prayed before getting out on the mat. *A winning wrestling team that prayed together? What a privilege it would be to attend that school!*

"I appreciate the scholarship," Larry told Mr. Hogue the next day, looking past him to the Wheaton College catalog on the shelf. "But . . . I was thinking . . . maybe Wheaton would be the place where I'd like to."

Dr. Hogue frowned. "Yes, well . . ." He wheeled around and pulled the catalog off the shelf, "Sort of a Bible school, isn't it?"

He leafed through the pages, frowning. "Well, if that's what you want, I'll check it out."

Unrelated letters from the principal, from Dr. Harold Strathearn at LeTourneau Evangelistic Center in New York, and from his pastor to Wheaton's President, V. Raymond Edman, resulted in a scholarship at a school distinguished as a training ground for the world's top Christian leaders. The future Reverend Billy Graham was a senior when Larry enrolled as a freshman on campus in September 12, 1942. Later schoolmates at Wheaton included three who became missionaries to Ecuador and were murdered by fierce Auca Indians: Jim Elliot, Ed McCully and Nate Saint.

In front of Pierce Chapel hung a large flag on which a gold star appeared each time a Wheaton man was killed on the battlefields of World War II. A war-conscious campus monitored the troop movements abroad and prayed for the far-flung fighting alumni of the eighty-two-year-old school.

The semester ground on and the war theaters grew hotter. A united nation prayed for peace, but continued to prepare for the bloodiest encounters against the Japanese expansionists and Hitler with his wild dreams of world conquest.

On December 7, 1942, all campus activities paused to mark the first anniversary of the attack on Pearl Harbor, which lead to the U.S. declaring war on Japan and formally entering World War II. Strong men began disappearing from class to join the allied forces. The voice of President Franklin Delano Roosevelt assured the youth of the nation that there was a place for them on the front lines, where thunder to thunder spoke. The nightly radio news brought grim reports from the South Pacific and the European theaters.

On December 14, Larry was eighteen—old enough to enlist. One month later, at the end of the first semester at Wheaton, he reported for duty in the United States Air Force (then called the Army Air Corps). He was assigned the number 32837111. In his farewell to college, Larry cried to God, asking for direction in this new life.

Early in his army career, he received an unexpected pass that would enable him to travel home. "Here's my chance to surprise everyone," he decided. Arriving at the Norwich Greyhound bus station, he walked a few blocks to his house. Peeking through the front window, he saw his mother sitting in the living room reading. Deciding to play it cool, Larry opened the door and strolled in.

"Hi," he said casually.

Orleva, equal to the occasion, calmly replied, "Hi," and then returned to her reading.

Larry stood there awkwardly, a bit crushed and not knowing what to do next. And then he saw the little smile playing at the corner of her mouth.

"Did you wipe your feet?" his mother asked.

Then came the cries of joy, the hugs, the tears, and the long visits to catch up on the news before Uncle Sam beckoned and it was time for him to return to the war.

Although Larry volunteered to join a squadron heading for Germany, his assignments in the military kept him in the United States and its Alaskan territory. After instruction as an aerial gunner in Nevada, he was sent to Ladd Army Airfield in Fairbanks, Alaska, and finally to a detachment in Watertown, South Dakota. In Alaska, days were short and nights were long for most of this mission. A bright spot was an abandoned library on the base. After a day of flying, even before he shed his flight suit, he would slip into the library and read. He fondly remembered the books available to a lonely gunner in a remote war.

In Watertown, South Dakota, one memorable morning always stood out in his recollections. His unit had been assigned to a training flight to practice air-to-ground firing. The men were instructed to try to bring the target down by firing at the base of a certain structure.

"But remember," the dispatcher intoned, "fire only off the *left* side of the plane. There'll be an abandoned red barn and white house near the windmill."

Larry suited up and crawled into the Plexiglas-covered tail of a bomber. Soon, he was roaring down the runway and lifting off into the blue for the firing practice run. Its altitude reached, the twin-engine plane banked and started down. Larry looked to the left. Sure enough, there was the abandoned farmhouse and the red barn and the windmill, which they were supposed to target.

Rat-a-tat-a-tat . . . the guns fired and his tracers were finding their mark beautifully. Funny thing, though, he noted that there were chickens running around down on the ground. He thought for a moment. Why were there chickens at an abandoned farmhouse? Oh, well . . . He had a job to do and kept firing.

Just as he took aim on the second pass, he felt someone pulling his leg. His first impulse was to keep firing and check later on what his buddy wanted.

The airman flying with him was pale. "S-stop!" he gasped. "We've got the wrong windmill!"

The farmer and his wife had dived under the bed at the first pass, but had managed to call the operations office only after three more attacks to stop their friendly enemy from pouring more lead into their "abandoned" farm.

With the maturing that came from his military service, Larry sensed the need for someone to share his life—someone with the same dedication and willingness to follow the ways of God. In Watertown, he enjoyed the unusual experience of serving, as the founding director of what became a thriving Youth for Christ rally program. He selected for his own place of worship the Christian and Missionary Alliance Church. A small decision, perhaps, but broad in its implications, for in that small congregation Larry found the sweetest person in his life—who was also gentle, patient, and well-suited to support him in his God-ordained career.

7

A HOME AND CAREER

A WEEK of special evangelistic services was planned at the Watertown Christian and Missionary Alliance Church. One evening, Larry returned to town after roaming the skies in a bomber over the Black Hills. He hurried into church and slipped into a back pew to enjoy the service.

He noticed with sudden interest the guest pianist whose back was toward the congregation. When the song ended and she turned around, his eyes widened and his heart stopped. Before him was the most beautiful girl he had ever seen. There followed the longest sermon he had ever heard, for his eyes were not on Evangelist Vance Berg, but on the back of the head of visiting Lorraine Hustad from Hibbing, Minnesota, the daughter of the former pastor in Watertown.

At the sound of the Amen, Larry zigzagged through the pews to the opposite side of the sanctuary and blurted out, "Hi, I'm Larry Ward."

Oh, no, Lorraine groaned inwardly, *not one of those obnoxious flyers at the air base.*

The soldiers, in the opinion of the Watertowners, had ruined their city. *At least he's in church*, she concluded, as she looked him over.

Lorraine had received her nurses' training at Luther Hospital in Watertown, so she was altogether familiar with the Air Base. When her parents moved to Hibbing on the famed Mesabi Iron Range, she moved there and found a position in a hospital, but had returned now to visit some friends.

Larry worked fast. He attended church every night that week. To a mutual friend, Mrs. Ila White, he confided one night, "I think she's terrific!"

"Well, you know, don't you?" Mrs. White whispered. "She's leaving tomorrow for Echo, Minnesota."

Larry quickly obtained a three-day pass, bought a ticket to Echo on the Minnesota and St. Louis Line, and boarded at the Watertown Station. As he walked through the train looking for Lorraine, he found her seated near the back of an empty car—the only passenger on the train. As he stepped in, he hurried to her side and asked, "Is this seat taken?"

The conductor punched his ticket, winked, left, and never returned during the entire trip except once to report that the engineer was stopping the train to clear the track. On the two-hour journey, the new friends spoke of many things—themselves, the Christian and Missionary Alliance, the war and finally . . . Grandma Hustad, whom he would meet at the end of the line in Echo.

Larry already knew other members of the Hustad family: Lorraine's parents, her pastor-cousin David, and another cousin, famed Christian organist and composer-arranger Donald P. Hustad.

"By the time the train stopped I was hopelessly hooked," he said. "I was ready to meet the matriarchal Grandma Hustad or anyone else who might have stood in my way."

Lorraine introduced her new friend and Grandma looked him over. "He's just a friend from Watertown," Lorraine explained.

"She says he's just a friend," Grandma reported to the family, "but I think there's more to it than that."

Selecting a girl from such a beautiful family was to Larry a "wonderful bonus." He wanted no casual affair. After that train ride, they were off and running. Under his pillow at the base went an encouraging letter from Lorraine and the photograph that was enclosed.

The date of July 5, 1947, was already affixed in the timetable of God's providence. After a year at Wheaton College, Larry took his campus (and military) buddy Bob "Old Sarge" Baker to Hibbing and proudly stood at the altar to receive his bride. He had never proposed and run the risk of receiving a negative reply. But, the actions of man are the best interpreters of his thoughts, so Lorraine had little doubted his intentions all along.

Lorraine Alice Hustad Ward had made her commitment to Jesus Christ at the age of eight years. An only child, she was reared in a quiet home free of tension or disunion. Her supportive attitude toward the ministry of Christ, her ability to endure her husband's long absences as he has traveled the world in missionary endeavors, her thrift, serenity, and home management made her the perfect mate for her nomadic man.

"What does a wife do when her husband follows the kind of work that keeps him away from home?" Lorraine reflected on their thirty-fifth wedding anniversary, "Some marriages survive, some don't. A wife must feel a part of the ministry. This kind of love requires a bit of courage and a bit of wisdom in handling the children."

Larry had been mustered out of the service on January 29, 1946. He had returned to a civilian life with a fiancée, a modest savings account, and hours of experience both in the work of war and of preaching the gospel. Since it was too late to enroll for Wheaton's spring semester, he had answered an urgent plea for help from an old friend and joined the staff of the LeTourneau Evangelistic Center in New York City. One of his assignments had been editing *The Joyful News*. There, his appetite for Christian journalism was sharpened. He sold his first published piece during that period. It was a tract titled, "Believing and Behaving," the subject for which arose out of a series of experiences in New York City.

While he was getting a haircut on Eighth Avenue one day, the barber remarked, "Your hair's getting thin. You ought to try our special tonic. No use losing your hair, young fellow."

Larry was impressed—until he looked up and noticed that the barber was a bald as a cue ball.

A little later on the street a newsboy called, "Extra! Extra! Read all about it! Paper, mister?"

"Well, what's the news?" Larry asked.

"How should I know?" the boy replied. "I never read the paper."

Larry stored away in his memory those two amusing experiences. They clicked because they occurred so closely together. Then, to make the series complete, he encountered a third on the next day. As he was studying a menu in the New York restaurant called "A Bird in the Hand," he asked the waitress what she recommended.

"Couldn't tell you," she replied. "I never eat here."

Larry remembered the story of the old preacher who told his congregation: "There are two things every Christian has to do. We have to believe the Gospel—and behave the Gospel."

The barber was talking about what his hair tonic would do, but he wasn't applying it. The newsboy was urging others to read the news, when he didn't bother to know what it was.

Larry's tract, "Believing and Behaving," was published in 1946, "full of all the clichés and corny expressions you can think of," according to the author, "but it must have had a message for the heart, because it went through several printings. Larry once recounted that, "A missionary in Africa found it in his Bible a few months ago and here and there I've heard preachers give those same illustrations in sermons."

In September 1946, Larry returned to his studies at Wheaton. He had heard that Robert Walker, editor of *His* magazine and of *Sunday Magazine* (which later merged with *Christian Life and Times* to become *Christian Life*), was teaching at Wheaton. Larry took all the classes he could from Walker and became satisfied that writing would be his major. This involved three semesters as editor of the campus magazine, *Kodon*.

"The only way to get an A in this class is to have something published," Dr. Walker told his eager young scribes.

The challenge was accepted. Larry secured his A when he wrote an article on "Unbelievable Bud" Schaeffer, a Wheaton basketball star, for *Power* magazine and another for *My Counselor*, both published in Chicago by Scripture Press.

By the next year of school, Larry and Lorraine were married. While carrying a full scholastic load, he served as pastor of the Michigan City, Indiana, Missionary Baptist Church (General Association of Regular Baptists), traveling the two hours by train every weekend with his bride, and on other occasions as he was needed. In addition, he accepted a position as Managing Editor of *Christian Life* magazine (alternating work days with Alvera Johnson, who was leaving the position to teach at Wheaton). Larry also took night classes in journalism two nights a week at Northwestern University's Medill School of Journalism, and later in layout and design at the American Academy of Art in Chicago.

William J. Peterson, editor of Eternity magazine, entered Wheaton College two years behind Larry.

"I walked into the office of *Kodon* magazine," William explained, referring to the campus literary journal, "and met the stocky, cheerful editor. Larry took me under his wing, encouraged me, counseled me, and bolstered me. Before I knew it, I was an assistant editor of the magazine. Larry had always been a great encourager. I was amazed that this upperclassman who was really a big man on campus cared about my future and me. Beyond that, he had a contagious excitement about Christian journalism. He was a tireless worker. He would go without sleep for seventy-two hours to meet deadlines and prepare papers for classes. How he remained so buoyant through it all, I can't say. Then he would sack in for twenty-four hours straight to catch up. He and Lorraine lived in a trailer behind the men's dormitory. One night just before a deadline on the campus magazine, Larry invited me over to meet Lorraine and share dinner with them. I will never forget the simple warmth of the home and the graciousness of Lorraine. When our oldest son Ken was born, Larry stopped in for a fortuitous visit. I'll remember always the way that Larry prayed for the baby, who was struggling for his life at the time. Larry cared, and you felt his caring."

Lorraine worked as a nurse at West Suburban Hospital, but she kept the coffee pot filled for Larry's campus buddies, such as Henry Pucek and Bob Baker, who made regular visits. With a full load of units at Wheaton, two nights of study each week at Northwestern University in Chicago, working three days a week at *Christian Life*, preaching each weekend in Indiana, editing *Kodon*, or in his own words, "doing anything anybody asked me," Larry faced in his last year of college one of life's most anguishing moments—the loss of a promised life.

"The miscarriage was a shattering disappointment," Larry and Lorraine recalled. Two kids in a trailer, a long, hard night, a kind neighbor's call for an ambulance . . . finally the trip to the hospital to make certain no infection would threaten the life of the mother. But the ordeal seemed far away with the appearance on June 16, 1951, of their next child, Sherilyn Sue.

As Larry's 1949 graduation day approached, the Wheaton faculty discovered that he was one unit short in the sciences. Larry enrolled for a semester of geology and went happily to the first class. "It was," he decided, "so terribly boring that I didn't go back." He read the textbook, went in on the last day, took the final examination and got a C. It was that grade which lowered him to "high honors" at Wheaton instead of the *summa cum laude* distinction.

In June 1949, after graduation, Larry turned in earnest to the things God would have him do. He had learned to trust his Lord for the future because he had seen God's fingerprint on the past. He had been weighing graduate studies in either journalism or theology, and considering a call to serve as pastor of a church in Indiana. But Larry was geared to meet needs. His friend and mentor Bob Walker needed someone at his side, and that was enough for Larry. The day after he graduated, he reported for fulltime work at *Christian Life* magazine as assistant managing editor and shortly thereafter took the full position.

Larry was famous at *Christian Life* for his speed and accuracy in proofreading the galleys. Once when he was away on a trip, he returned to a happy staff that had just put the next edition to bed at the printers. When Larry picked up a set of proofs, they assured him, "You have nothing to worry about. They've been read and reread and all corrected."

Larry let his eye travel down the galleys.

"Hey, don't you trust us?" his associates pouted.

Pretty good job . . . until he came to the last galley. There he spotted a paragraph, which read: "Don't miss the follow-up article in the next issue by our managing editor, Larry Lard."

A quick stop-press call to the printer corrected most of the issues, but thousands were already packaged and gone, to give subscribers a good laugh.

8

GOD'S SYNCHRONY

THE WORLD for Larry Ward during his stint in the offices of *Christian Life* on Wabash Avenue in Chicago's Loop was growing wider. The film *China Challenge*, distributed by Youth For Christ Evangelist Bob Pierce, had piqued Larry's interest in missions and in the wider world of Christians' responsibility.

Perhaps that's why a small notice in the *Chicago Tribune*, which he read one morning in 1951 on the commuter train from Michigan City, Indiana to Chicago, caught his interest:

> *"U.S. Government wants persons for exciting experience abroad. Need journalism background."*

Larry folded the paper and pondered the matter. The idea of travelling abroad as a missionary at the expense of Uncle Sam appealed to him. Back at the office, he sent a note asking for an application.

Several days later, he received a phone call inviting him to the Conrad Hilton Hotel for an interview. On the day appointed, he entered the lobby and found it full of hopefuls like himself. Thinking he had little chance, he waited for half an hour or so, watching the men and women enter and leave in a steady stream. He was about to leave when his turn finally came.

"We're forming an agency called 'Voice of America,'" the officer in charge explained after an hour or so of interview. The longer they talked, the more Larry warmed to the assignment. His journalism credentials and experience were especially appealing to the government, along with his high moral standards. The salary was high, the benefits plentiful. He was told there would be something like 120 days home leave each year.

"You're the kind of man we're looking for," his interviewer finally said. "Fill out these papers and bring them back in a week. A special committee will be coming from Washington to interview you."

Larry left thinking he was on his way, but in the week that followed, he sensed in his heart a growing check against accepting the assignment. Finally, on the day of the appointment, he went in early to the office. He put the sheaf of papers on his desk and wrote his name on the first line as directed. Somehow it just didn't look right to him. He had arranged to take the day off, but he phoned the Voice of America office at the Hilton and told the contact person that he would not be applying. He tried to explain, but his reason fell awkwardly on unhappy ears, "I just feel God doesn't want me to do it," Larry explained.

As he hung up the phone, his secretary buzzed, "A Doctor Ketcham is waiting to speak to you," she said, "Doctor Robert Ketcham of the General Association of Regular Baptist Churches."

"We've been trying for some time to organize a publishing house for our association," the caller explained, "but we don't know anything about this sort of thing. Is it possible you could get away today and come over to give us some advice?"

Larry was confident that God had timed the call . . . and somehow he knew at once that his happy days at *Christian Life* were winding down and that a new opportunity was upon him to serve the church group in which he had found the Lord.

As Director of Publications for the GARBC, Larry began to travel almost immediately. He visited churches, talked to Sunday school leaders, interviewed Christian education directors, and became acquainted with pastors. With travel came joy and fulfillment as well as some disappointment—and often, God's unexpected synchrony. Larry loved his work.

A break came in 1954 when Larry, as editor of the official periodical *The Baptist Bulletin*, disagreed with an article Dr. Ketcham had written which was critical of Evangelist Billy Graham. Larry had a profound admiration of Dr. Ketcham, and respected his right to his own opinions. But, he insisted such an article should be identified from a personal viewpoint and not appear to represent an official GARBC position. (The association itself had taken no specific position on Graham and his crusades).

Larry also had differences with his GARBC brethren because he was not the extreme separatist many of them were. For Larry, the emotional ties remained strong. He had surrendered his life to Christ in a GARBC church in Norwich, New York. He had been licensed to preach by the GARBC at fifteen. His father was a GARBC preacher. The people in those churches loved the truth and stood for salvation—and in that, he could definitely join them. But, he also felt they often attracted bad press they didn't deserve, because they let a vocal minority speak for them.

In a meeting in Los Angeles, the council of fourteen of the GARBC sided with him indirectly. In fact, they offered to create a new position for him where he would become the official spokesman of the GARBC, and they encouraged Dr. Ketcham to use his gifts of preaching in the sunset years of his ministry at Bible conferences.

Larry was thirty-one years old. He felt honored to have this invitation from the General Association of Regular Baptist Churches. But, he felt that God wanted him to remain in California, even though he didn't know exactly why. He only knew that it was time for him to move on. In February of 1955, he submitted his resignation to the GARBC. It was accepted, but with the request that he continue in his work until June 1.

Meanwhile, in a totally unrelated development, Larry had written to an old friend—Dr. Cyrus N. Nelson, President of Gospel Light Publications—suggesting that a publisher such as Gospel Light should issue a magazine for Sunday school teachers. Larry actually proposed the specific content for such a periodical, giving it the working title of "*Teach.*"

This led to a continued communication with Dr. Nelson and a letter to Larry, which stated: "Gospel Light as a matter of policy doesn't hire people away from other organizations. But, if you decide that you yourself would like to pursue that idea for a magazine, we would be open to talk with you about it."

In still another seemingly unrelated development, Larry and Lorraine received the startling news that the property on which their house was situated in Hayward, California, had been condemned for a city parking lot. This led to a legal hassle.

Returning from the board meeting in Chicago where he had resigned from the GARBC and had accepted the request to stay on until June 1, he found two bulky envelopes awaiting him. One was a specific job offer from Dr. Nelson. It stated: "Come whenever you like. We have discussed it here, however, and the ideal date for us would be June 1."

Larry blinked, and then breathed a silent prayer. Even the date seemed to be a confirmation of this move as part of God's will.

He opened the second letter. It was an official document, telling him that a check in a certain amount had been deposited to his account in the bank, and that this completed the purchase of his home. The letter stated: "But as a mark of good faith and to show our desire to cooperate, even though your house is now officially ours, you are free to stay there free of rent or other charge until June 1."

"It always seems that God deals with me this way," Larry would say, "I guess He knows that once I know I am really in His will, I can move ahead with total confidence. So He seems to underscore it for me, as He did with these three items which all converged on that same day, June 1."

Larry and Lorraine, with little Sheri and Mother and Dad Hustad, purchased two houses and a garage on half an acre in Montrose, California, just north of Glendale. Larry took the job as Director of Education Services for Gospel Light Publications. The year was fun, relaxed, and rewarding. The Wards enjoyed Montrose, and after Larry's four years of heavy pressures, constant travel, and long days away, they found a special benediction in evenings at home together unaccompanied by a briefcase full of extra work.

Larry loved his colleagues at Gospel Light and was privileged to serve with them in a sort of "transition" period. He also took the first steps to get *Teach* underway and spent a great deal of time in evaluating other periodicals and publications of Gospel Light and making long-range proposals.

But Larry was about to hear the beat of another drum.

As he walked into his office one morning in early 1956, an unmistakable feeling swept over him that was as clear as if an audible voice had said, "Your work here is ended."

He sat down a bit shaken and propped his elbows on his desk. What was this? Lorraine and Sheri and the folks were all happy in this place. His job was very rewarding. The salary was adequate.

"*If I left,*" Larry reasoned, "*what would I do? Work on a magazine?*" But then he asked himself, "*What magazine?*" The voice inside him continued to push. How about a "*missionary society?*"

In the middle of his reverie, the phone rang, "Larry, this is Carl Henry. I don't know if you remember me or not, but I'd like to ask you some questions. I'm not at liberty yet to tell you why, however."

Eventually, Dr. Henry explained: "We're thinking of publishing a new periodical. Your name has been suggested as managing editor." Carl went on to explain that they were not thinking of a person to be directly involved in the content planning of a new periodical, but to take care of the mechanical aspects of production.

Larry promised to think it over, and Carl thanked him warmly.

Leaning back, Larry thought through what his answer would be if Dr. Henry ever did call him back. His several years of directing the Regular Baptist Press had broadened his outlook and experience. At Gospel Light, he had been involved in studies related to advertising and promotion and marketing in general. To return now to the limited work of production after all these broader areas of experience seemed unappealing. He reached for a clean sheet of paper on his desk and wrote:

1. Editorial production
2. Circulation promotion
3. Advertising solicitation

Larry slipped the note under his telephone and returned to the work of the day, thinking that if Dr. Henry did call back, he would just read the material from this note to explain his broader base of experience and why the limited responsibility of production would not be sufficiently challenging.

Now the thought had at least entered his mind that perhaps the Lord was planning for him to move forward. At home that night, Larry discussed the turn of events with Lorraine, "If I had my choice of where to live," he said, "I think it would be Washington, D.C. That would be a fascinating place."

The next day, he drove to the post office to look at the listings of available government jobs. Somehow the Lord seemed to be prying him loose from his position in Glendale, one finger at a time. A couple of weeks later, he answered a call and found Carl Henry's voice on the line again. Larry reached under the phone and pulled out the sheet of paper on which he had listed his reasons for not accepting the job.

"Well, Larry, the job I spoke of earlier has broadened a bit," Carl said. "I don't know whether or not you will be interested. It now covers three areas instead of just one—editorial production, yes, but also circulation promotion and the entire advertising program."

Larry listened in amazement, looking at the paper in his hand as Dr. Henry, without knowing it, quoted almost verbatim the list he had prepared.

Then a letter from Billy Graham followed, urging Larry to take the position with the new magazine.

"I have followed your career for years," Billy wrote in essence, "and I think you're the man to help us get this new magazine started."

The magazine would be called *Christianity Today*, a periodical to serve as a counterpoint to the liberal *Christian Century*. Location? The offices would be in Washington, D.C.

On his get-acquainted trip to Washington, Larry could easily see that the other editors (basically theologians, preachers, and writers) were outstanding in their own areas, but they desperately needed the help of someone experienced in actually putting a magazine together. He was asked to travel to New York City to be looked over by J. Howard Pew, the oil magnate who was financially backing the periodical for its first years.

The tycoon opened his suite door at the Waldorf Towers (atop the famed Waldorf Astoria Hotel) to admit Larry, and took a puff on his cigar as if to say, "You're not quite what I expected," turned around, and let Larry into another room. After Mr. Pew had asked a preliminary question or two, Larry surprised himself by taking the initiative. "Pardon me, sir, but I'd like to ask you some questions."

J. Howard Pew laid down his cigar, blinked, and peered at him as Larry queried, "You're putting up a lot of money for *Christianity Today*. What does this mean? Are you going to dictate the editorial policy?"

Mr. Pew blinked again, looked at Larry for a moment, and then leaned back and smiled. Somehow, the atmosphere of the interview changed. Mr. Pew answered the question frankly, and to Larry's satisfaction.

Looking back on that interview, Larry wondered how he had mustered the gall at the age of thirty-one to say what he did to such a famous executive. But, the pleasant conversation that followed rewarded him, and Larry greatly appreciated his further contacts with Mr. Pew throughout his career at *Christianity Today*.

The Wards leased their Montrose house for the promised year of work—April 1956 to April 1957—moved to the capital, and Larry plunged into the heavy load of editorial work. The demands were so great, the hours so long, and the pressure so intense that a skin rash appeared on Larry's arms. The loss of sleep and the relentless demands of editorial production, advertising solicitation, and circulation promotion were also taking their toll.

Automobile trips with Lorraine and Sheri through the Shenandoah Valley, the Skyline Drive, and the strategic battlefields of the Civil War provided weekend diversions. As they were passing one Saturday afternoon through Front Royal, Virginia, Lorraine exclaimed, "Did you see that sign?"

"What sign?"

"Back there, that historical marker?"

Larry put the car in reverse gear and backed up along the curb to read a message that would have far-reaching implications. It said something like this:

> On May 23, 1862, the Maryland First Regiment CSA opposed in this village the Maryland First Regiment USA. Believed to be the only time in the Civil War in which the divided halves of a single regiment fought each other.

Larry surveyed the peaceful streets, the well-kept houses, and the manicured lawns of the city park. "Right here," he said, "brother battled brother . . . people who looked alike, who were raised in the same communities . . . boys who knew each other, shooting and bayoneting each other . . ."

He shook his head to get rid of the thought. For the first time in his life, the Civil War took on an atmosphere of reality, instead of just being dull history.

That night in a motel at Winchester, Virginia, he bought a book chronicling the battles of the area—the battle of Front Royal, and of Newmarket, where youthful students of the Virginia Military Institute (ages twelve to fourteen) were strapped into their saddles and thrust into the war.

"It reads like fiction, but it was real," Larry commented to Lorraine and little Sheri.

In the weeks following, the idea of a novel formed in his mind. He read all he could get of the life and times of Stonewall Jackson and learned that the great Confederate general was a committed Christian believer. Larry ground out his story of two brothers, one in each half of the Maryland First Regiment. Finally, the dreaded day would come when they must face each other in battle on the streets of Front Royal.

In October, just as the first issue of *Christianity Today* was to appear, Larry got up extra early one morning to write a prologue to what would become his first novel, *Thy Brother's Blood*. "Old friend fired at old friend," he penned, "ex-comrade drew sword on ex-comrade—and brother battle brother . . ."

In Larry's view, what he had written was really just an extended outline for the great historical novel that he would write "someday," when he had time to finish it. But then, caught up in the pressures of issue after issue of the new magazine, the manuscript gathered dust in his desk and finally went with him back to California.

That was in 1956. In 1961, with the centennial of the Civil War's start only months away, Floyd Thatcher of Cowman Publication phoned Larry to have lunch.

"If I were a publisher," Larry reflected, "I'd really get on the bandwagon of the Civil War. There's going to be a lot of interest. Floyd, why don't you bring out a great Civil War novel?"

"Okay," Floyd replied, "why don't you write it?"

Larry reached into a bottom drawer of his desk, pulled out a faded manuscript in a ragged box, blew off the dust, and handed over *Thy Brother's Blood*.

Shortly after that, he left for an extended trip outside the country. Opening his mail in Japan one day, he found a flyer announcing the coming publication of the civil war novel, *Thy Brother's Blood*, by Larry Ward, the story of Stephen and Wade Andrews. It was the story of a house truly divided with one brother in the gray uniforms of the Confederacy and the other fighting in the blues of the Union army. It would be issued on the Centennial Anniversary of the beginning of the Civil War.

Thy Brother's Blood deserves rereading, if only to understand Larry Ward better. The two brothers, Stephen and Wade, were on opposite sides in more ways than one. Stephen was a Christian; Wade was not. In the last scene of the book, after the two had met in the heat of battle and (at the insistence of Stephen, the Christian) had actually fought each other, the character, Wade, explains what finally brought him to faith in Christ. One step was when he met Stonewall Jackson, whom he described as "a real man."

The most convincing thing to Wade (as quoted earlier) had been the example of his own brother, a man *"to whom truth was truth so much that he would pick up a gun he hated, and kill men he loved—and even fight with his own brother."*

That is the same dedication to truth, which always marked the life of Larry Ward.

His year at *Christianity Today* had been another great experience for him. He kept his commitment to work away at those three jobs until each area had a full-time person to direct it. But now, although he was offered even broader editorial service opportunity at the new magazine, his heart told him that God had other—perhaps different—work ahead for him.

Right on schedule the Wards returned to California. Lorraine, Larry, and Sheri—each with a keepsake first edition of *Christianity Today* in their suitcases—made their way West, back toward home, toward Grandpa and Grandma Hustad, toward new and exciting endeavors in the center of God's will for them.

9

WORLD VISION

IN HIS SPANISH-STYLE white house under the stately trees on Briggs Avenue in Montrose, California, Larry cleaned out a closet and put in a desk. On December 14, 1957, he would be thirty-three years old. His promised year at *Christianity Today* had ended, as had his earlier stint at Gospel Light Publications. Larry Ward was finally a free agent.

Even though his desk had been narrowed, his world in 1958 would stretch beyond the 700 churches of the GARBC, the 60,000 subscribers of *Christian Life*, the domain of Washington, D.C., and the new voice for the evangelical faith, *Christianity Today*.

Shortly before leaving Washington to return to California, Larry had talked with Dr. Frank Phillips, whom he recognized as the hard-driving chief executive of a missionary agency called World Vision, Inc., based in Portland, Oregon.

"Larry," said Dr. Phillips, "I hear you'll be going to Cincinnati next month for the convention of the Evangelical Press Association. Roy Wolfe, one of our staff guys, will be going too. He's kind of reserved. Would you look out for him?"

Roy, a veteran of the art staff at the *Oregonian* newspaper in his home state, was seeking an editor for the publication, which would eventually become *World Vision Magazine*. But Roy didn't mention his mission to Larry in Cincinnati. The two talked about generalities, ate Chinese food, and enjoyed the EPA program. Afterward, Larry returned to Washington, while Roy went to Chicago for an interview with Dr. Robert Walker. When Roy mentioned he was in search of a top-drawer journalist, editor Walker scratched his head. "Well," he pondered, "you might ask Larry Ward. I've just heard that Larry will be leaving *Christianity Today*."

In the Mayflower Hotel of Washington, D.C., at a convention of National Religious Broadcasters, Frank Phillips asked the same question of *Christianity Today*'s news editor, George Burnham. Just then, George spotted Larry standing nearby. "There's your man!" he said. "Larry, could you come here a minute? Frank here is looking for an editor."

Larry smiled. "I appreciated your thinking of me, Frank, but I'm pretty well settled in the Los Angeles area with several accounts and probably couldn't move to Portland."

"You're behind the times, Larry," Frank said, laughing. "We've just moved to L.A.—1101 West Colorado Boulevard in the suburb of Eagle Rock."

"That's about six miles from my house," Larry said. "I'll come in to see you next week."

Back in his room, Frank took a call from Roy in Chicago. "I've got an editor for us," Roy reported.

"I beat you to it," replied Frank.

"Who's yours?"

"Larry Ward."

Roy chuckled. "That's *my* man, too!"

Until this time, World Vision to Larry Ward had been just Bob Pierce, a big, red-faced Youth for Christ evangelist who toured the country showing films of Asia and taking offerings for the needy. The closer Larry got to the organization, the clearer the opportunities became. He worked for several months as a consultant, testing the waters, watching God's clock. He was enjoying all of his accounts, but somehow World Vision was beginning to consume most of his time and creativity. Larry was thrilled about its potential.

One late afternoon, December 7, 1957, he pulled a piece of stationary out of his suitcase in the offices of his client, World Vision, and wrote a note to Frank:

You've always said to me if ever I wanted to go full time all I had to do was to notify you. Well, if you want me, here I am.

Frank, bubbly and excited, phoned as soon as he received the message. "It's all arranged," he exclaimed.

One month later, Frank Phillips suffered a fatal heart attack on the steps of an airplane at Los Angeles International Airport. The timing of that note had been strategic. Larry couldn't have known when he wrote it how urgently Bob Pierce would need someone to move into the entire area of promotion.

The months went by, and Larry swiftly transitioned from serving as an editorial consultant, into the big (though as yet untitled) job of coordinating all of World Vision's information and fund-raising programs. He appreciated Roy, and all his colleagues at World Vision. This happy association was enhanced by Lorraine's announcement that a second child would be born in August of 1958.

In order to clarify in their minds the scope of World Vision's projects, to capture need in thousands of photographs, and to lay the groundwork for expanding missionary projects, Larry and Roy had planned a trip that would take them around the world. A travel agent delivered the proposed itinerary, with its strange-sounding names, just in time to complicate the happy announcement.

"You'll be leaving," Lorraine pointed out, "three days after the baby is expected."

"Then I'll cancel," Larry declared.

"How can you?" Lorraine replied. "You've got all your hotel reservations, all your flights arranged."

"Honey, if you want me to cancel, I will," Larry insisted. But, Lorraine was equally insistent.

On August 6, 1958, Kevin Charles Ward was born right on schedule. And also right on schedule three days later, Larry and Roy departed on an SAS flight for Copenhagen, the first leg of their momentous trip.

Did the lack of bonding between father and child in those early days and months affect their future relationships?

"We've thought about it a lot," Lorraine would say later. "Today we live near both of our children and have the sweetest relationships any parent can hope for. Kevin, in his growing years, when Larry was traveling so much, did have my father living in an adjacent house. Dad provided the male companionship that Kevin needed. Kevin loved Grandpa so devotedly that he even began to walk like him, limping a bit just as my dad did."

Both parents would agree that Sheri suffered most from her father's long absences during her teen years. But, the early associations of family living and a strong church home helped. They were enough to bring her full circle into an adult life of very active Christian service.

When he wasn't writing appeal letters, news releases, photo captions and copy for brochures, Larry was giving time to the larger strategy of World Vision, Inc. He categorized the thrust of its endeavors into five basic goals: (1) Social Welfare Services, (2) Evangelistic Outreach, (3) Christian Leadership Development, (4) Emergency Aid, and (5) Missionary Challenge.

He conceived the idea of offering, with no rental fee, World Vision's new film, *A Cry in the Night* to churches that, in turn, promised to take up an offering for *their own* missionary outreach. The plan (despite early misgivings by Bob Pierce) was an instant success in promoting the services of World Vision nationwide.

Early breakfast appointments, after-dinner phone calls, and heaps of mail dominated Larry's schedule at home, in the office, and on the traveling circuit. Sandwiched in was the work of the Evangelical Press Association, now a decade old. Larry had agreed in 1958 to develop the weekly EP News Service, both to serve EPA's member editors and to garner needed revenue for the association's program. He created and named the bi-monthly *Liaison* newssheet, which would present information and announcements of interest to the editorial family. He also wrote the yearly "Religion in Review," directed "Protestant Press Month," attended board meetings, traveled to host cities to plan conventions, and arranged for grants from World vision to strengthen the base of EPA, which served a group of Christian editors widely diverse in responsibilities and theological viewpoints.

"As I told Bob Walker on a train back there in 1948," explained Larry, "I consider that experience with EPA—serving the field to which God called me—one of the greatest privileges of my life."

I received a phone call from Larry Ward in July 1958. He asked if I would write the weekly EP News Service while he was overseas on that first globe-circling trip. The "account" was a glamorous one for me in my pint-sized freelance writing career in Long Beach, California. I had been married for just two years and relished the opportunity to broaden my responsibilities. These grew broader still on November 2, 1958, when I drove up to 1101 W. Colorado Boulevard at Larry's invitation. Just as I parked my Ford across from the tiny annex, out stepped Larry Ward and Roy Wolfe from their postage stamp quarters.

"I have to admire these guys who show up for work precisely at coffee break time!" Larry teased. That was my first indication that I had the job.

During the coffee break at Bob's Big Boy restaurant, we turned over the table napkin and outlined the second issue of the new *World Vision Magazine*. Such a periodical is routine now for missionary agencies, but in those early days, it was indeed a phenomenon. Response was voluminous.

The very first issue had been put together toward the end of that world trip in several countries of Asia. Larry wrote the copy in Manila—but where could we have the type set in English? A patient search led to a Chinese printer with English type who would set the galleys and provide glossy proofs, which could be pasted down for the printer's camera. Because of the language barrier, Larry and Roy could discuss with him the printer's jargon only through patient negotiation. While Roy stayed in Manila to get the proofs, Larry went on to Taiwan, where they would later meet.

Proofs in hand, Roy landed in Taipei and started to lay out the proofs, page by page, in that hot, humid climate. All he needed were the usual tools: a board with a straight edge, a T-square, a ruling pen, a jar of rubber cement, and some cardboard on which to fasten the layouts so they would not get bent or wrinkled between the drawing board and printing press.

The only T-square available was of a strange variety with graduated sides sloping from its wide mount on the crossbar to a tapered end. Unless the layout was turned, all the lines of type on the page would go downhill. The only ruling pen was a left-handed type that wouldn't let the ink flow smoothly. And the only "rubber cement" available was a kind of white glue. Finding no table to accommodate his layout, Roy had to use the lid of a toilet seat—the only flat surface in their improvised production shop half a world away from the office in California.

"Those were the fun years," Larry recalled. "Roy and I believed in the program and gave ourselves to it wholeheartedly. It was gratifying to see the response."

In Larry's tiny British-built Austin-Healy Sprite, he would often pick me up in neighboring La Cañada and we would cruise through the early morning fog, make our way into the new location of World Vision offices at 117 East Colorado Boulevard in Pasadena, and brainstorm yet another edition of the magazine or tackle a different editorial project. Still long before the office crew arrived, would come the shout from Larry, "Hey, let's get some coffee and a couple o' doughnuts . . . take a break."

The budget for World Vision, Inc., in 1957 was $750,000. Larry and Roy saw their efforts produce steady fruit over the next three years. The following year, it grew to $2,068,000. By 1960, it stood at $2,668,000.

In 1962, toward the end of the year, Larry walked into his office and once again met that strange urge that the time had come for a move.

"Roy, come in here a minute, will ya?" he phoned.

There followed an outline of a plan to take their skills to a variety of worthwhile smaller agencies, offering to handle their total promotional package. Roy Wolfe's response: "Why not?"

The new information agency was called "TELL Services," taken from the Lord's admonition to his disciples, "Go and tell." Larry opened an office on Oceanview Avenue in downtown Montrose near his house and he and Roy set to work. As the news filtered out, agencies sought their services without their needing to advertise. In the typical Ward brand of generosity, no advice or counsel was ever withheld. All his life, Larry had quite naturally helped writers and editors—even preachers—find places of service in the work of ministry. Over and over again, he found jobs for the unemployed and stood by his friends.

But Larry did not fare well in the overburdening pressures of the two-man shop. The buck stopped at his desk, and that desk demanded more hours than he had. The work was there, but the office was too small. The knowledge was available to share, but Larry's servant heart was taxed beyond its ability to handle the possibilities.

In the fall of 1964, two years into TELL, the doctor diagnosed the trouble: angina pectoris. Larry prepared either to die or to become a vegetable. Roy meanwhile, for family reasons, had decided to move back to Oregon. So TELL Services, despite its successful beginning, was dissolved.

"One last trip," Larry told his wife. "Let's take one last trip together."

They went 150 mile east to Palm Springs for several days of complete rest and relaxation. A bit more hopeful, Larry returned home and began leafing through his mail. A letter from Wheaton College President, V. Raymond Edman read:

Dear Larry:

I was thinking about you today… Thought you might like to have this year's verse from Wheaton…

Larry picked up the enclosure. It read, "For I know the plans I have for you," declares the Lord, "plans to prosper you and not to harm you, plans to give you hope and a future" (Jer. 29:11, NIV).

Larry fastened his attention on the last few words: "to give you a future and a hope." He read it slowly, read it again, and held it in his hand as he walked around the room.

"Suddenly I felt the joy of the Lord flowing through me. A future and a hope, not as a vegetable, but one full of hope, plans of welfare, not of calamity." Larry felt the strength of the Lord flooding through him and knelt by the living room sofa to thank God for the promise. When he got up from his knees, the pain in his chest was gone. It never returned. Larry accepted it with joy even though he would say, "I don't fully understand it. I just accept it from the Lord and praise him."

Twenty-four hours later, his comrade in mission, Bob Pierce, phoned Larry. The two men hadn't spoken for two years since Larry had announced this decision to leave World Vision. Larry had written Bob notes from time to time, but the break was clean. Bob had never replied.

"Hi, buddy," Bob began. "I've just been thinking of you." His voice was slow, faint, far away. "I've been remembering some of the visits we had here together. Larry, we need each other. God bless you. I love you."

At the end of the conversation Larry sighed. "What a gift of God *that* was!" he told Lorraine. "If I die today, I'll be happy because any misunderstanding between us has been cleared up."

The next day was the date for an appointment with his Wheaton pal and confidant, Henry Pucek, and an attorney. The plan was to start a missionary agency and to become active again in world missions, which Larry had come to love. But a court schedule forced the attorney to cancel the lunch, and Larry was available to talk when Bob Pierce called him back that day. This time his speech was not slow, but alert and full of authority.

I've got a proposal," Bob asserted. "Now don't answer until you've thought this through."

Lord, help us! Larry groaned. *World Vision is the one place I wouldn't want to go back to. Here Bob and I have just worked things out and now I'll blow it.* But, Bob pressed on and twenty minutes later, Larry's attitude began to change. *Well, why not?* He was prepared to accept Bob's invitation. *I'm free, and we aren't talking about forever*, he thought.

"I know just the job and the title I want you to have," Bob continued. "Come with me buddy. Come back and work with me."

On April 4, 1965, Larry wrote a letter of resignation to the EPA board of directors. The flow of services to member periodicals had dried up while he was out of the country. He wanted to give the position of executive secretary to someone new. The time had come to provide his full attention to the work of Bob Pierce, a man whose vision and creativity made more of an impact on his Larry's life than any other single individual, a man whose heart was broken by the things that break the heart of God.

Bob Pierce was a complicated man who knew his faults, believed that "God don't owe me nuthin'," and was prepared to give every ounce of strength for Christ and his Kingdom. That was the kind of dedication Larry could respect, and the kind of man to whom he could unhesitatingly give loyal service.

10

BOB PIERCE

THEIR TWENTY-YEAR association had begun in an unlikely way. Larry drove to 1101 W. Colorado Boulevard in Eagle Rock that April morning in 1957 for his first appointment as a part-time publicist. Bob had just completed an unpleasant management duty.

Larry found Bob to be a man with a driving burden for the lost, an evangelist with tireless compassion for the widows and fatherless of the world, and a man with reckless generosity toward friends and servants of Christ around the world. In the years of their association, they worked, traveled, prayed, laughed, and wept together. They stood on the borders of closed-off China, where it had all begun for Bob Pierce in 1947, and they wept as they echoed the dying cry of Francis Xavier for the China (Cathay) of his day: "O rock, rock—when wilt thou open to my Lord?"

They walked through the wall-to-wall children of Korea . . . the crowded streets of Tokyo . . . the bloody battlefields of Indochina . . . the hungry masses of Kolkata . . . the breathtaking vistas of Nepal . . . and forbidden areas of northern India where almost no other foreigners had been allowed to go.

"I always operated on the fact that if it's breaking God's heart and you do what you can about it, God will make up the difference," Bob would say. "I have always called the difference between the utmost that a man could do, even with access to the greatest brains and the greatest science in the world, *God room*. The difference between that one-third and the two-thirds that God wants done is called *God room*. Everything else can be explained away. Man can take credit for it. Nothing is a miracle until it begins with *God room*."

Larry heard those words nearly every day of his life as he remembered his departed friend.

On Larry's office wall in Scottsdale, Arizona, he kept a color picture of Bob Pierce. Larry's associates knew he would always sit so that Bob's picture was in front of him. "If I have five people in my office for a meeting, there are really six. Bob is there, too," Larry would say.

Bob Pierce was a month away from his sixty-fourth birthday when God took him. Bob had moved among kings and presidents. He had ministered to thousands in a great evangelistic crusade in Asia, and to millions in North America via radio. What began with one little homeless girl placed in his arms by a distraught missionary became multiplied 100,000 times over through a child-care program he initiated.

Born In Iowa in 1914, Robert Willard Pierce grew up in humble circumstances in Los Angeles. He made his commitment to Jesus Christ as Lord and Savior at the age of twelve. Immediately he became an evangelist on street corners, as well as in one-to-one contacts. He attended Pasadena College but did not graduate. He was married in 1936 to Ruth Lorraine Johnson, daughter of Dr. Floyd B. Johnson, a pastor and evangelist. He spent some time in itinerant evangelism, and then joined his father-in-law in pastoral and radio ministries.

The year 1944 was a turning point. Bob met Torrey M. Johnson, who, with Billy Graham and others, was forming an organization called Youth For Christ. Bob directed the Seattle YFC rally, and then hit the road later with the Eureka Jubilee Singers, an African-American ensemble.

And 1947 was an even bigger turning point. Bob went to China under the auspices of YFC and discovered a new world: Asia, the Orient, millions of people, the developing world, with incredible need and suffering. It was a place that needed the healing, helpful, "right now" touch of Jesus Christ.

In September 1950, Bob joined YFC leader Frank Phillips in forming a new organization. Appropriately, and reflecting his own enlarged spiritual vision, it was named "World Vision, Inc."

Bob Pierce inspired Larry. Their close association lasted until 1967. Larry had become Vice President/Overseas Director and stayed on after Bob resigned to organize The Samaritan's Purse, which he directed while battling leukemia until his death in 1978.

In 1974, at the International Congress on World Evangelization at Lausanne, Switzerland, Bob Pierce introduced Larry to a gathering of clergymen and missionaries from all parts of the world with the fondest of words:

> *"Now, I want to tell you something. Larry Ward traveled with me for twelve years. Many of the things that have been written over my name, Larry Ward wrote every word of 'em. That's a fact. Any place it says Bob Pierce, evangelist, author, et cetera, you can depend on it, about 99 percent of everything worth reading Larry wrote. God bless him.*
>
> *He loved me enough to help create that illusion that I was somebody, and I love you for it, Larry—but the wonderful thing is that now one of the first men who moved into Bangladesh when other people were just thinking about it, a man who was there in minutes, almost, was Larry Ward. And he's loved by the head of state, by the man there who is in charge of relief for the whole government. Larry Ward has just been his backbone, and now he's in the midst of all this suffering in Africa.*
>
> *There are literally shiploads of food right now docking there, and other shiploads on the way—tons and tons of food going into the starving areas of Africa because Larry, the minute he heard about it when he had to borrow money (I'll betcha—and I haven't asked him, but I'll bet he had to borrow money). If not, he put it on his credit card and asked God to help him before the bill came. But*

he went out and he got something going, and that's the characteristic of these two, Larry and Lorraine. God bless Larry Ward!"

Larry's skill in editorial communication had given a new dimension to the element of authority and compassion that characterized the life of Robert W. Pierce.

Top: Portrait of Larry Ward, painted by his artist-father, Whitney Ward.
Bottom Left: Proud member of the Norwich High football team, Larry's first love.
Bottom Right: Larry and Lorraine at their wedding reception.

Top Left: Larry during his military stint in World War II.

Top Right: Larry Ward

Center: Larry helping to direct relief operations in Guatemala.

Bottom: Larry and Lorraine visit with Mother Teresa in Kolkata.

Top: Larry leading kids in "Go Dodgers!" cheer.

Center Left: Larry visiting children in Africa.

Center Right: Larry with a little friend in Korea.

Bottom: Larry visiting with children in Cambodia.

Top: High up on the roof of the world, Larry visits Lake Titicaca, Bolivia.

Center: During a rescue of Vietnamese boat people, Larry helps lift up the anchor as the Food for the Hungry mercy ship starts its voyage into the South China Sea.

Bottom: Larry Ward (left), receives Cross of Merit from the Order of St. John by His Royal Highness Prince Peter of Greece and Denmark (middle), with Henry Pucek, FH Board Chairman (right), observing.

11

"IF YOU DRAW OUT YOUR SOUL TO THE HUNGRY . . ."

BY 1970, Larry's mission had taken him millions of miles through more than sixty countries. Often, he would meet with World Vision staff members and visit projects in one country by day, then board an airplane and sleep in his clothes en route to the next country and a new set of responsibilities.

Then he would carry back to North America the missionary challenge which he would use in speaking engagements, telling what still needed to be done for the poor and suffering. Larry found the words of Jesus blunt and direct regarding a believer's responsibility to the destitute, so he had no reluctance in asking for help.

A speaking tour of Canada took him finally to Toronto in April 1970, where he was invited to appear on Elwood Glover's daytime television show, "Luncheon Date." When the red light of the camera came on, Glover told the audience, "Ten months out of every year, the man beside me walks through a very different world from the one we know here in Eastern Canada. Today, he's going to tell us about it." Then, turning around to his guest, he said abruptly, "What's the first thing you think about when you think about that world?"

Larry paused for a second, then replied: "I see an old woman beside the railroad tracks in India. She looks like she is starving to death—and the baby in her arms could already be dead."

How strange of me to say that! Larry thought. But he hurried on, "I see a little girl in Laos, hungry . . ."

When the red light went out, Glover shook his head. "Man, you're really informed about the issues of world hunger."

Larry mumbled something in response, but all the way back to his room and into the night he pondered those words: "world hunger . . ."

A week or so later, back in his own house in California, he dreamed that he was looking into the faces of the 12,000 people who were at that time starving to death each day. He awoke shouting, his voice ringing through the house.

Strange, he thought.

The words of Dr. Richard C. Halverson, chairman of the World Vision board of directors, kept coming back to him. Larry remembered how his friend Dick had spoken strongly in a board meeting about "the world's biggest problem in the years ahead: hunger."

In Japan, on the way home from troubled Laos, Cambodia, and Vietnam, Larry was temporarily stranded for a day before he could board his flight home to the United States. He checked into the airport hotel at Tokyo, planning to dictate reports and correspondence related to his trip. The growing burden for a hungry world kept intruding, interrupting his thoughts, and demanding attention. He tried reading his Bible, but found concentration difficult. He laid his Bible down and knelt beside his bed in prayer.

"About all I could do in my prayer," he said later, "was admit to God that the great overwhelming burden for a hungry world—which so long and so slowly had been forming in my heart and mind—had now suddenly crystallized into something specific, sharp, prodding."

Getting up from his knees and sitting at his hotel desk, Larry tried once more to resume his work. He pulled toward him the Bible he had been reading and continued where he had left off. The words of the next verse seemed to reach out and grip him with paralyzing strength.

"And one of them . . . stood up to predict by the Spirit that a great famine was coming."

The prophecy was specific in its context, but for Larry, the passage of Scripture had a larger meaning—a call to involvement, a kind of confirmation that a new direction had entered his life. He could not know at that time that the burden would mean a change in his life's work, leaving an organization with which he was happily engaged to move out alone in the vast frightening stretches of the hungry world. He did the only thing he could think of, which was to kneel down beside his bed and pray. "Here am I, Lord, send *me*."

In Kolkata, a few weeks later as he checked into the Lalit Great Eastern Hotel downtown, he was moved to share his growing concern about world hunger with his former associate, Roy Wolfe. That message on tiny gray stationery was the first formal crystallization of his burden to concentrate on feeding the hungry, a mission that few agencies at that time were carrying out with any regularity or emphasis. The message read:

"I owe it to you, Roy, to enlarge on my thinking a bit . . . although in so doing I must not cramp your own objectivity and creativity.

I visualize: (1) an all-out campaign, alerting Christians to world hunger and informing them of their special responsibility. (2) An all-media information program, including a magazine—a "Fotomagazine." We gave the world MAP Miniature Magazine. This new format, which no one is utilizing, would be all photos. (3) Public speaking (churches, schools, service clubs). With unusual visuals and sound effects. (4) Articles and releases. (5) Direct mail, of course. (6) Public service advertising. Maybe at least related to "World Hunger Day" or to our use of Thanksgiving. This includes public service radio and TV spots. (7) A film—twenty-one minutes, no narration. Music and effects. Each year, Thanksgiving will be especially utilized.

All that is just the beginning. The program itself includes development of a "World Food Bank" (which is really just a computer showing available food reserves worldwide), emergency aid, development of pilot projects and food factories worldwide—including scholarship grants—and cooperation in long-range technologies research (really just a computerized list of research projects in action).

The Emergency Aid aspect features local-level projects as well as money. (In the spirit of our Lord's words, at the feeding of the multitudes: "Give them something to eat yourselves." They had offered money!)

I am in process of listing every verse in the Bible dealing with this subject. What an eye-opener! (And heart-opener.)

Well, there she is . . . in great confidence to you alone. (No one else has heard the full version.) What think ye? Please write about this when you get time, busy buddy. Thanx."

On each flight from then on, Larry would scribble a note to Roy on the unlikely stationary of airsickness containers and mail them to Roy at the Seattle Times.

"I'm ready to give my life to this as Frank Laubach did to literacy. Five years from now, the starvation problem in the world will be so big and real that most of our other problems will be seen as the trivia they are."

In another note written aloft Larry confided:

"Years and years of burden and heartache all have come to a special focus—the hunger problem of the world.

I found myself preaching it over and over during a recent three-week swing of Canada. I have studied this thing—am writing a book using the words of Jesus, "I Was Hungry" as the working title.

Twenty, thirty years from now, things could be better. There are 48,000 scientific projects underway, trying to make foods out of non-foods as well as to increase food production. But tomorrow, ten thousand people now alive will be dead from starvation. Technology can help long range. But now—this year, next, for the next five or ten or fifteen years—the only answer lies in sharing, and the logical people to whom to tell this are the Christians (whose Lord was blunt and specific in his instructions)."

One airsickness bag reflected back on that first world trip he took with Roy:

"You know, just twelve years ago right now, you and I were pushing around out here; twelve years later, the job still isn't done. The doers (Lil Dickson, Mrs. Donnithorne, etc.) are all older and very few new doers to be seen."

On September 1, 1970, only a few weeks before he would resign from World Vision, he wrote from Seoul:

"Seems to me, Roy, that one of the things I must study is the complex matter of national economics vs. humanitarianism concern. Hundreds of thousands starve in India while grain enough to feed them all is stacked high on the plains of Alberta . . ."

And four days later, on a flight from Phnom Penh to Bangkok:

"Yesterday, I visited a Cambodian refugee center. Heartbreak. Little kids dying of dysentery—because they are so weakened by long-term malnutrition. Others with all the telltale signs of protein deficiency. And ahead for Cambodia—a possible serious food crisis. The areas that have supplied much of the food are under Communist control, so this can be a very critical time. Good meetings with the Ministers of Health, Social Welfare, and (re: refugee housing) Public Works . . ."

On the last leg of his journey home he wrote a brief note to Roy on an Air Vietnam motion sickness bag. The last line of the message read, "I feel as though I am embarking on the biggest mission of my life."

Flying back to Nairobi in a small plane after visiting famine areas in northern Kenya, Larry scribbled these lines for me on a notepad:

Pray with Our Tears

Hungry and hurting,
Ready to die;
Hungry and hurting,
Please hear my cry.

Forty thousand children
dying every day;
Is anyone listening
To hear us when we pray?

Hungry and hurting,
Trying to hide our fears;
Hungry and hurting,
Praying with our tears.

Forty thousand children,
Too weary to have fun;
Forty thousand children,
Dying one by one.

12

"THEY DIE ONE AT A TIME . . ."

"But Jesus said, 'You feed them'" (Mark 6:37, TLB).

IN SEPTEMBER 1970, Larry submitted his resignation to the World Vision board of directors just after he had received a raise in pay. In his new mission, he would work for two years without a salary. His was not beginning with small plans. He was prepared to pay the price of venture.

A man is not simply defined by what he has done, except perhaps in the case of Lawrence Edward Ward. Larry did not ride horses, collect stamps, play golf, tennis, or even checkers. There seemed no greater recreation to a man who lived for others than to tackle the impossible—such as a family planning program for Kolkata, or a water purification project in Africa, or a radio/television series calling affluent Americans to pay attention to the needs of his adopted people.

In 1970, World Vision invited a roomful of Larry's closest friends in Pasadena for a dinner celebrating the beginning of his new work. The agency presented to him the first gift—a $25,000 grant with which to purchase food and ship it.

Every move Larry ever made professionally had been a step backwards in terms of salary, but God always made up any lack: from *Christian Life* to the General Association of Regular Baptists; from the top editorial position with the GARBC, to a slot in the editorial mills of Gospel Light Publications; from a top editorial position with *Christianity Today* to freelance work; from working with many clients to just World Vision, Inc.; from a secure, well-paying position, to finally no salary at all.

To prepare at age forty-five for a new career with a single focus and a sharpened vision, Larry read over several small libraries. Among the first soul-wrenching volumes (there is nothing casual about world hunger) was the account of a British Methodist missionary to Africa.

"The other day a Zambian dropped dead not a hundred yards from my front door," wrote Colin Morris in *Include Me Out* (London, Epworth Press, 1968). "The pathologist said he'd died of hunger. In his shrunken stomach were a few leaves and what appeared to be a ball of grass. And nothing else."

The experience, Pastor Morris wrote, stabbed his conscience awake. "Two thousand years of Christian history were blown away by the faint sigh of that little man's last breath....He died without knowing that Jesus cared for him, not in a sentimental, spiritualized way, but by the offer of a square meal."

Other books which Larry sampled and digested in those days included: *The Hungry Planet*, by Georg Borgstrom (Collier); *Famine in Retreat?*, by Gordon Bridger and Maurice de Soissons (Dent & Sons); *The Black Book of Hunger*, by Josué de Castro (Beacon); and *Overcoming World Hunger*, by Clifford M. Hardin (Prentice-Hall). One that especially touched him was *The Social Conscience of the Evangelical*. It was written by Dr. Sherwood E. Wirt, then editor of the publication Decision, and later to become a valuable member on the board of directors of Food for the Hungry.

In 1973, Larry wrote *...And There Will Be Famines* (Regal Books). In the forward, Billy Graham hailed it as a book "to quicken the social consciousness." The book ends with the observation: "They die one at a time . . . so we can *help them* one at a time. And we must."

The origin of that phrase is traced to the early days when the call first came to Larry to dedicate his remaining life to the feeding of starving people. He was driving on a Hollywood street, praying aloud, "just talking with God as [he] drove along," and the devastating thought of more than ten thousand people dying each day from starvation or malnutrition weighed heavily upon his soul.

But Father, he prayed, *what can I do? I'm just one person . . .*

An answer that was audible only to the ears of his heart struck him as clear as a bell: "But they die one at a time, my son, *they die one at a time.*"

Larry slowed his car, pulled over to the curb of Franklin Boulevard, and stopped. With his head bent over the steering wheel he prayed, "Thank you, Lord. If they die one at a time, then we can *help* them one at time."

And he did.

After his resignation from World Vision, but before its effective date, Larry, with his son Kevin at his side, went traveling across the Pacific. Anxious that both Kevin and Sheri understand his motivations in leaving World Vision, a work in which they had shared his deep personal interests, Larry had determined to let eleven-year-old Kevin help him find a name for the new work into which God was calling him.

"Kevin," said Larry, "you and I are a special committee to find a name for this new work."

Together they sat writing various words: world, food, hunger, and so on. Suddenly, on the Continental Airlines flight, a flight attendant came by to serve lunch. Beside each plate was a small, colorful card, which the airline had thoughtfully provided as a "grace before meal."

"Kevin," said Larry, "Let's read this before we pray."

The words were from Psalm 146. As Larry read aloud, he suddenly came to these words: "I am the Lord who gives food to the hungry."

They looked at each other, startled.

"Dad!" exclaimed Kevin. "That's it! Food to the Hungry!"

"How about, 'Food *for* the Hungry'?"

"Great!" Solemnly father and son shook hands, and Food for the Hungry has been, ever since, the appropriate name for the work Larry began.

It was also appropriate that the name came from the Scriptures. Like the Bereans, Larry searched his Bible to learn what it had to say about hunger. He thought he knew the Scriptures, but suddenly there were more direct, piercing orders from the Creator to feed the hungry and to share with the needy than he had ever seen before.

Early in the work of Food for the Hungry, launched in January 1971, Richard Dalrymple of the *Los Angeles Herald Examiner* interviewed Larry for an article. He wrote, "I suppose you have looked into the faces of more hungry people than any other man of our day. I guess that's why you are doing what you are now, to begin such a work to help the hungry."

"That's part of it," Larry admitted. "I would not want to look into all those hungry faces and not be moved." But now he reached out and held up his Bible. "Actually, it was not so much looking into all those faces as into this book which gave me the incentive for what I am doing."

And this was true. Following the example of his own father, who learned to search the Scriptures, Larry had gone to the Bible to find out what he was supposed to do. He was particularly concerned about the priorities of his own life. Those long years before, at LeTourneau Christian Center in New York, he had dedicated his life to Christ. He knew this meant that he would have to share the love of Christ and point people to the only Savior of the world. He didn't want to be sidetracked by secondary issues.

But is helping the hungry a secondary issue?

Larry didn't think so. He often said that his study of Scripture convinced him that God's love reaches out not only to the whole world, but also to the whole man. God cares about every aspect of our lives.

Larry's Bible was marked throughout with the letters "S J" in the margin. They stand for "social justice," which Larry felt was the bedrock of all that Food for the Hungry was endeavoring to do.

Among the verses so marked in his Bible were these:

"If I have hurt the poor or caused widows to weep, or refused food to hungry orphans . . . or if I have seen anyone freezing and not given him clothing, or fleece from my sheep to keep him warm, or if I have taken advantage of an orphan because I thought I could get away with it . . . let my arm be torn from its socket! Let my shoulder be

wrenched out of place! Rather that than face the judgment sent by God" (Job 31:16-23 TLB).

"He who shuts his ears to the cries of the poor will be ignored in his own time of need" (Proverbs 21:13, TLB).

"You must love and help your neighbors just as much as you love and take care of yourself" (James 2:8, TLB).

There were dozens and dozens of such verses marked in Larry's Bible. He often thought about compiling them into a special condensed and topical scriptural booklet.

Events began moving rapidly in 1971. Larry's Wheaton College buddy, Henry A. Pucek, retired from the Conciliation Court in Los Angeles, rented an office twice the size he would need in the Los Angeles suburb of Eagle Rock and shared the space and rent with the new agency. A board of seven directors assembled for the first time on January 25, 1971. Attorney John Caldwell drafted the incorporation papers for the new organization. Computer genius David Tuttle (one of those first board members, "a visually handicapped person with incredible vision") offered helpful organizational counsel.

In sequential board meetings, Larry charted the organization's steady growth. One of his earlier trips was to the "new" (at the time) nation of Bangladesh (formerly East Pakistan). He was convinced, as he stood at the battered airport in Dhaka early in 1972, that he had gone there "in the will of God." All around him were the ravages of war. Bangladeshis, on whose backs the people of West Pakistan for so long had grown rich, had only a few hours earlier organized their own government as the newest (and eighth largest in population density) nation in the world. Larry felt keenly the incredible harmonization of God's purpose in bringing him to the scene at that critical hour.

"But there I stood," he recalled, "scared to death. All alone. Empty-handed. Ready to run. Some three million people had died there the year before. Ten million who had walked a trail of tears to India were now coming home in rags and poverty, many of them to find their homes destroyed and their villages obliterated. Tall grass covered all traces of previous habitation. An additional twenty million Bangladeshis could be classified as displaced within their own country."

Larry looked at his watch. Despite the whisper of the Holy Spirit he had heard back at home, he thought, *Well, nothing I can do here. Might as well catch the plane to Kolkata. This is too big for me.*

Four hours later, he was sipping tea there in the capital city of Dhaka in the house of the new president of Bangladesh. God arranged it after Larry made one visit to the house of Cal and Marion Olson, missionaries with the Assemblies of God who had stayed on through the dreadful nine months away. Their lives had been preserved, but they had been robbed at gun- and dagger-point.

Larry spent most of 1972 in Bangladesh, specifically working in connection with a massive airlift directed by his friend Russell O'Quinn, a pilot who had flown help to Biafra in the earlier crisis. "The program was not without its problems," Larry recalled, "but well over twenty million pounds of rice were carried to the needy." (This was also the point at which Tippi Hedren, Hollywood actress and star of Alfred Hitchcock's *The Birds* and other movies, joined the ranks of Food for the Hungry as a tireless overseas volunteer, distributing food in disaster situations, serving on the Food for the Hungry mercy ship in the South China Sea, and living for weeks in a tent on the Cambodian border).

The need for an airlift had been one of the special concerns that Larry had taken to the U.S. after his meetings with the Bangladesh officials. Russell O'Quinn had been one of the first people he called, along with Dr. J. Raymond Knighton of Medical Assistance Programs (MAP) and Dr. Viggo Olson.

In fact, Larry had called every agency that he could think of, appealing for them to move in to help Bangladesh with all its need. A particular concern was the estimated 200,000 women who had been raped by the invading soldiers of West Pakistan in what the president of Bangladesh described to Larry as "a deliberate program of national humiliation."

Just as 1972 was passing into history, there came another disaster: the earthquake in Managua, Nicaragua. Within hours, Larry was on his way there to research the needs firsthand after the massive earthquake had killed more than 8,000 people and rendered some 365,000 homeless in just a few seconds of midnight terror.

Again Larry had seen God's wonderful timing. Strong headwinds had delayed the little plane in which Larry was riding to Nicaragua with his friends Dr. C. Mervin Russell, Dr. Hal Stack, and Kenneth Stroman. But, arriving with providential timing in the middle of the night, they were taken directly to the presidential palace. The young man who just "happened" to meet them in the middle of the night was the nephew of the president, and they were not only able to assess the needs, but to make arrangements so that every ounce of the 405,000 pounds of food shipped into Nicaragua by Food for the Hungry would reach the Christian workers for whom it was designated and who in turn would pass it on to the neediest of the needy.

In the months that followed, Food for the Hungry continued to send help to Nicaragua. In July, a phone call from Washington, D. C. brought a message from the office of Doug Coe and the international prayer breakfast movement: "Doug phoned in from Romania. He has just been in Africa—wanted to know if you have any plans to be there. He especially wants to urge you to go to Mauritania."

Larry looked at his desk and shook his head in wonderment. Sitting there was a recently delivered ticket to West Africa including a stop in *Mauritania*. Earlier that same day, Larry had told his travel agent: "Pearl, work out whatever you can for Senegal, Mali, Niger, and Upper Volta. But whatever you do, make sure I get to Mauritania. My instincts tell me it has to be the hardest-hit area (with the least help) in all the Sahel."

Ten days later, he had surveyed the needs and was hurrying home to rally help, to plead for food and funds. But a late arrival in Paris caused him to miss a plane. He would have to waste many hours and spend the night. Apparently, he and his fellow passengers would lose valuable time.

"Well, Lord," Larry sighed, "guess I can't complain. Your timing has been so perfect these past few weeks."

Larry thought back to his earlier conversation with an agnostic pilot friend named Hank. Hank had scoffed when Larry competently predicted before the trip began that God would be going ahead of them to prepare the way. "Hank," said Larry, "mark my words. You are going to see things happen in the next two weeks, which defy all the laws of chance and probability. You are going to see how God is timing our trip minute by minute and step by step."

Later that first day, as they flew toward Africa, Larry had read these words: "Oh, how great is your goodness to those who publicly declare that you will rescue them" (Psalm 31:19, TLB).

"Well, Lord," Larry had sighed, "I guess that's what I have done. I have publicly declared that you are going to rescue us!"

Now, there in Paris, he was waiting and praying when suddenly a bus appeared. *A bus? Just for my friend Hank and me? Just for the two of us?*

No, just before the bus pulled away from the curb, an African gentleman hurried aboard.

"You have come far?" he asked casually, arranging his baggage.

Larry nodded. "From Mauritania . . . place called Nouakchott."

The man whirled around in delight and astonishment. "Then you must be Dr. Larry Ward of Food for the Hungry! I missed you in my country and wondered as I flew here today how I could contact you. I am the Ambassador of Mauritania to the United States. I have wanted to talk to you about the needs of my country and how you can help."

Hundreds of thousands of pounds of food were rushed to desperate people in Mauritania, because of that "chance" meeting with a remarkable man, the distinguished ambassador.

In January 1976, Larry stopped in Guatemala City to meet with Captain José Umberto Fuentes Soria and his associates in disaster relief coordination.

Larry asked, "What plan do you have for evacuation and feeding in the event of a major earthquake or volcanic eruption?"

The man smiled, "Dr. Ward, there is little chance of that here. We don't have earthquakes in Guatemala. But yes, we do have a plan."

They produced that plan, and the meeting continued with specific discussion on how Food for the Hungry could cooperate in the event of a major disaster. That same day, Larry appointed the Rev. Isai Calderón as honorary director of Food for the Hungry/Guatemala. He also phoned his office in the U.S. to order an immediate food shipment.

Three weeks later to the day on February 4, 1976, Guatemala City was hit with one of the most devastating earthquakes in human history. But Food for the Hungry had already shipped in 65,624 pounds of food, had already established top-level contacts, and already had its own infrastructure in place. The agency could put its relief goods in honest Christian hands for effective person-to-person distribution.

Through constant travels, endless meetings, voracious reading, writing reports, speaking and seizing every opportunity to learn, Larry spearheaded the steady expansion of Food for the Hungry into agricultural research, dramatic water-purifying projects, hydroponics, irrigation, mud stoves, solar cookers, harnessing of the wind, and catching and using rainfall in simple dams and cisterns. He led in the purchase and development of the Desert Center (a unique research and demonstration facility that used to stand near the former Food for the Hungry office in Scottsdale, Arizona). He also challenged his associates to develop the International Hunger Corps, a division of Food for the Hungry that trained and deployed volunteers from across the globe as well as the United States.

In addition to initiating the Desert Center in Arizona, he also sparked development of an experimental ranch in Mexico for finding appropriate technology in tropical agriculture; and the raising of an urban agricultural center in India, seeking ways in which every flat rooftop and every corner of a room can be turned into a source of food. Larry never pretended to be a technical expert. He would explain, "I just see the needs out there and 'holler' for help." He paid grateful tribute to his colleague, Dr. Dean Nauman, who had designed most of the innovative development tools, such as solar cookers and the "Hope House" emergency shelter.

With his colorful colleague, the Senior Vice president Dulal Borpujari, Larry sparked Food for the Hungry participation in unusual seminars and workshops abroad. The agency had teamed with the Food and Agriculture Organization of the United Nations (FAO) to co-sponsor international workshops in Malaysia, China, and the Philippines on such subjects as "preserving the rice harvest" and "utilization of agricultural wastes for energy in rural food production."

Larry was a compassionate voice to "plead the cause of the poor and needy." But his strong interests in development, in helping people help themselves, led to the establishment by Warner Southern College in Florida of the "Larry Ward Chair of International Development." This began in the fall of 1983.

In between emergency trips abroad at times of sudden disastrous calamities or to combat creeping devastation and desertification, he also hammered out the concept of internationalization. Larry directed the establishment of Food for the Hungry's International Coordination Center in Geneva, Switzerland, and with it the International Institute for Relief and Development (I.I.R.D.).

The I.I.R.D. would provide fellowships and scholarships honoring people who had served the poor and hungry of the world, offer intern field experience, fund and participate in special undergraduate and graduate study programs, arrange international university exchanges, utilize the help of specialists as "On-Call Fellows," maintain a resource library, and produce various training materials.

It had specific hunger awareness tasks, such as an annual listing of the "hungriest nations," the sponsorship of conferences and workshops on critical issues, special publications including the *Hungry Nations Yearbook*, news briefings, and special tours for writers and editors.

"I regard the Institute as one of the most significant ventures into which God has ever led us," Larry would explain. "We had the privilege of being something of a pioneer in the field of helping the hungry. Other fine agencies were doing that as *part* of their programs, but to our knowledge, we were the first to be directly operational with this as our one specific goal and purpose, the one string on our guitar. Now we are moving on into another pioneering area, and I believe that the establishment of the International Institute for Relief and Development is fully as important as the beginning of Food for the Hungry itself."

Joining Food for the Hungry as Executive Vice President and Director of the I.I.R.D. at this time was Dr. Homer Dowdy, a college contemporary of Larry's at Wheaton. He was an experienced editor and writer, author of several missionary classics, as well as a leading newspaper editor, and for years an executive and eventually Senior Vice President of Charles Stewart Mott Foundation, one of the leading and most prestigious philanthropic organizations of its kind in the United States.

"Homer is a gift of God to us," Larry would explain. "We were honored that he had chosen Food for the Hungry for this, and then even more so when he agreed to come on board with us in a full-time position."

"Imagine," said Larry, "a Christian board sitting every three years in Geneva sponsored by the International Institute for Relief and Development, talking not only about the problems but also about the solutions, pointing to appropriate technology that is practical, educating through videotape, lectures, seminars, and workshops, publishing books and periodicals and 'how to' pamphlets, stocking a library of up-to-date monographs prepared by specialists in every discipline and by people of God who can expound the Scriptures and put the message of the Bible into perspective for this generation."

God's synchrony had become a way of life for Larry. It allowed him to sleep well at night, content to let God be God in the ordering of his daily work.

Larry was deeply grateful for the donors who made possible all the ministries of Food for the Hungry. "We're just a switchboard," he would often say, "connecting people on this end who care and share with the desperate needs out there. Here are people I don't know personally, people who don't know me except from the mail or TV, but they trust us to be their hand to help the hungry. What a sense of responsibility that gives us."

At the time, 85 to 90 percent of Food for the Hungry income was sent in "a few dollars at a time" by the general public, Larry and his associates would pay special tribute to their friends who periodically helped with large gifts for special needs. In addition to many such individuals, they mentioned especially the organizations headed by Pat Robertson, Jerry Falwell, David Mains ("Chapel of the Air"), and Val Hellikson and Paul Evans ("Haven of Rest").

"Pat, for example," explained Larry, "has periodically come through with just the right amount needed at that time, often without any special appeal from us. He must really have his antenna up and pointed in the right direction and must really be responding to the Holy Spirit's guidance because the perfect timing has been incredible. We are most grateful for people like this, who have their own big programs to support, but who stretch their hearts to help us help the hungry and homeless."

13

A LIFELONG LOVE AFFAIR

"IF YOU COULD CHOOSE where you were going to die, what place would it be?"

We were traveling together somewhere in Asia once when I put that question to Larry Ward. Without the slightest hesitation he answered in one word: "Vietnam."

I always suspected that Larry, while answering, might have remembered many of those times when he looked death in the face in Vietnam during its "thirty years and thirty days of war."

Perhaps he was remembering the note he wrote to Lorraine in the dying hours of South Vietnam, in 1975: He penned, "*By the time you read this, I will have been officially listed as dead or missing. Don't worry. It is all part of a plan. Unless you see incontrovertible evidence that I am dead (such as actual identification of my body) or some official notification from North Vietnam that I am a prisoner, just trust God that I know what I am doing—and that this had to be done.*"

To Larry Ward, this was no foolhardy adventure. He loved his family, and ached with lonesomeness at the moment he wrote those words. But his great love for Vietnam and a deep (and, he felt, God-given) concern for the Americans missing in action were what prompted his very deliberate move to help the Vietnamese and missing Americans.

Vietnam was just one of many countries that Larry visited on his first trip around the world with Roy Wolfe in 1958. But it was a case of "love at first sight," and that love was to become a lifelong affair. To Larry, Vietnam had always been one of the most beautiful places in the world, with its lush tropical settings, hundreds of miles of sparkling beach, and, above all, the rugged beauty of its Central Highlands.

But to a "people-person" such as Larry, its real beauty was its people.

There were, of course, its missionaries, primarily from the Christian and Missionary Alliance (CMA) and later the Southern Baptists and Assemblies of God. Larry unhesitatingly described them as "some of the greatest missionaries in all the world, some of the most wonderful people I have ever met."

One of the first people he met there was John Newman, missionary with Overseas Crusades who was working closely with the CMA. Years later, John would play a large role in Larry's continuing efforts to help Vietnam by serving on the Food for the Hungry mercy ship rescuing Vietnamese boat people in the South China Sea.

Through John, Larry and Roy on that first trip met Herb and Lydia Jackson, pioneer missionaries to Vietnam who had been the first to carry the Gospel to the tribal people (dubbed "Montagnards" or mountain people, by the French). Larry explained, "I have no words in any way adequate to describe Herb and Lydia. Herb is one of God's noblemen and in Lydia he has a wonderful counterpart."

And through Herb and Lydia Jackson, early in his days in Vietnam, Larry met a remarkable man named Sao A, who was to become the subject of the book *The Bamboo Cross*, written by Dr. Homer Dowdy. Sao A himself was to have a special influence on Larry's life in later years, especially through his sons Ha Johnny and Ha Jimmy. And, as mentioned before, Homer Dowdy was to become a valued colleague, the executive vice president of Food for the Hungry and director of I.I.R.D.

On one of those first excursions to Vietnam, Larry visited the jungle leprosarium operated by the Christian and Missionary Alliance. He came away deeply burdened for the people serving there (especially Dr. Eleanor Ardel Vietti) and for the missionaries in nearby Ban Me Thuot, particularly Bob Zeimer, whom Larry remembered as a "rugged man's man." (It was Dr. Vietti, captured on May 30, 1962, who was to symbolize for Larry his burdens for the American missing and later also to represent those hundreds of "MIAs", the missing American servicemen. And Bob Zeimer would die at the hands of the North Vietnamese when Ban Me Thuot was overrun in 1968).

There's no way that Larry could begin to list all of the missionaries whose devotion to Christ and courage in a difficult situation impressed him so much. There were people like Grady Mangham, field chairman for the CMA in Vietnam, Pastor Gordon Cathay of the International Church in Saigon, and Dick Pendell in Can Tho.

But a very special relationship developed with a man named Dr. Garth Hunt. It was Garth Hunt who knelt beside a wounded Vietnamese serviceman, and who with tears in his eyes pleaded with Bob Pierce and Larry Ward to start a flow of crutches and wheelchairs into Vietnam, a war marked by people maimed by land mines and grenades. And it was Garth Hunt who would appear, driven by the constraining love of Christ in those last hours of Vietnam to stand by Larry's side as they coordinated the exodus of hundreds of Vietnamese in the last days of April 1975. Garth went on to become a member of the International Board of Directors of Food for the Hungry.

There were other very close ties: two of Larry's most beloved friends where Reverend and Mrs. Jacques Mottu of Switzerland. He was the pastor of the Église Française in Saigon, serving the French community there. The Mottus stayed on after the Communist takeover in April 1975, until they were expelled fifteen months later. After they returned to Switzerland, they stayed active in the work of Food for the Hungry, Jacques serving as a key advisor, and Madeleine spent time as secretary of the International Board of Directors.

While the Ward family lived in Hong Kong in 1969, they developed a close friendship with Mrs. Esther Fitzstevens, whose missionary husband John was another of Larry's special friends in Vietnam. (The Fitzstevenses also went on to serve with Food for the Hungry in Switzerland, with John as Vice President/Administration in the Geneva office.)

Those were difficult days in Vietnam and the friendships forged in the midst of the suffering were to last forever. Larry was very close to the staff of World Vision in Vietnam during his days as Vice President/Overseas Director of the organization, and held special ties with Director Doug Cozart and with Relief Director Melvin Van Peursem, whom Larry regarded as one of the bravest men he'd ever met. He kept warm memories of the colorful Dennis Dickerson, a British-born entrepreneur/contractor, who built the World Vision complex in Saigon.

In context of a war where travel was only possible through the help of the U.S. government with its planes and helicopters, Larry made many life-long friendships among the American servicemen, such as Chaplain Warren Withrow and Lieutenant Jim Meredith. In one of those special circumstances, which seem to characterize Larry's life—what he called "God's marvelous timing, the synchronization of is purposes"—he encountered a young pilot named Floyd Olson. Larry happened to be placed in Lieutenant Olson's bunk in Pleiku while the flyer was off flying a mission. He noticed Bibles and Christian magazines, among them a copy of the Wheaton College alumni magazine. Later, the two met and a warm friendship developed between Larry and the young Floyd.

It happened that Olson had been assigned to his own plane, supervising control tower installations throughout Vietnam. He and Larry were able to make many trips together up and down the country in Floyd's little "Beaver," fellowshipping in Christ and sharing some unusual experiences (such as being fired at by a Viet Cong sniper off the edge of the Ban Me Thuot Airport).

When Larry talked about the MIAs later in his life, it was always clear that those feelings were still very close to him. As for the helicopter pilot Floyd Olson, who voluntarily returned to Vietnam the second time as Captain Olson, he remains one of the 2,491 for many years listed as "missing and unaccounted for" in Vietnam.

Larry also had opportunity to develop many close friends among the Vietnamese themselves. Some of his contacts were with the highest officials of the land, who remained his staunch friends throughout his life.

One of these was the Deputy Minister for Refugee Resettlement, Nguyen Van Chuc (formerly the general in charge of all engineering operations for the Republic of Vietnam). Larry's desire to help the Chuc family escape from Vietnam was the first link in the chain that formed the eventual exodus and sponsorship of more than 1,800 refugees. Chuc himself, after a miraculous escape from Vietnam, joined his family in the unique "Hope Village" sponsored by Food for the Hungry in central California in 1975. General Chuc served as the camp director, and was a strong right arm to Larry there.

Another very special friendship to Larry was that with Reverend Doan Van Mieng, president of the Evangelical Protestant Church of Vietnam. They had frequent contact during Larry's many visits to Vietnam with World Vision, and later after Food for the Hungry began its operations in Vietnam in 1973. Larry will never forget Pastor Meing's heroic decision to stay in Vietnam in the face of the certain Communist takeover.

Larry first visited Vietnam in 1958, and returned several times in following years.

In March 1965, he and Dr. Bob Pierce with Joe Gooden began a series of survey trips for World Vision, laying the groundwork for the massive programs of relief assistance, which the organization was to eventually bring to Vietnam in some of its darkest hours.

From March 1965 until November 1970, Larry Ward was in Vietnam for part of almost every month—traveling through the battlefields, visiting the hospitals, meeting with government officials and church leaders, and counseling the World Vision staff as the programs developed.

His love for the country did not end when his service with World Vision was terminated. In June 1973, he returned to Vietnam to set up the country's first relief programs of Food for the Hungry and was there frequently the remainder of that year and in early 1974.

As the end of the war neared, he returned to Vietnam in November 1974 and was there almost constantly until April 1975. The U.S. had succumbed to political and media pressures, and had withdrawn its troops in 1972. The defenses of South Vietnam were beginning to crumble before the steady onslaughts from the north. His friends were in trouble and Larry was going to stand beside them. What happened in those last days is related in Chapter 16 of this book. What is worthy of mention here is the fact that Larry's love for Vietnam did not die when South Vietnam succumbed.

When opportunity came to return to Vietnam in August 1979, he jumped at the chance. This was the first of a series of eighteen trips over the next four years to set up significant assistance programs in Vietnam, especially for needy and handicapped children. It is doubtful that any other American official or otherwise, journalist or relief worker— was ever afforded the same opportunity for this kind of continuing contact with the post war Vietnam. For Larry, it was simple. It was still Vietnam, a country and people he loved. These were his friends.

And his love affair continued.

14

"WHERE ONLY MAN IS VILE"

LARRY FIRST GAZED upon the beauties of Vietnam in September 1958, midway through its "thirty years and thirty days" war. "Like two rice baskets at the opposite ends of a carrying pole," that is the way the Vietnamese describe their country, which uncoils in the form of an elongated S for more than 1,200 miles, from the ninth parallel north to the twenty-sixth, covering 127,300 square miles. Vast expanses of lush vegetation and endless rice fields stretched the metallic mirror of their flooded surfaces to the horizon during the rainy season, or presented the velvety green of growing rice at other times, breaking like waves upon the bony central highlands called the Annamite Cordillera.

Looking down upon beautiful Vietnam from planes and helicopters during his many mercy missions there, Larry often quoted the phrase from the old hymn, "where only man is vile." He was especially reminded of these words in early 1968.

With the storm of fire, the Tet offensive struck Saigon (now called Ho Chi Minh City) and other major cities the first week of February 1968. Larry was working at home in the U.S. when suddenly a telecast was interrupted by the news that the Viet Cong had reached the guarded walls of the U.S. Embassy in Saigon and engaged the Marines in a bloody battle. To do that, Larry knew they would have had to cross the grounds of the World Vision compound right next door. He wondered if Doug and Linda Cozart and their children were safe.

Larry grabbed the phone and called Pan American World Airways. "All flights to Saigon have been canceled," he was told. "We are over-flying until further notice."

Complicated legal matters would be in question across the seas in Saigon. Stockpiles of valuable relief goods were in danger. Above all, the lives of his colleagues were threatened. All these pressed upon him the need to go immediately into the eye of the storm.

His bag packed, Larry phoned Bert Perry, the young son of World Vision board member Coleman Perry, who had been looking for a chance to accompany Larry overseas. With Saigon still closed, they quickly booked a flight to Hong Kong, where they were told again, "All flights to Saigon are canceled, and there are long waiting lists." So the indefatigable Larry made his way to Bangkok, hoping he could talk his way onto a military plane if no commercial flights were available.

His first contact in Bangkok was with the U.S. Embassy, but he didn't find it all that helpful. Larry tried to explain the urgency of the situation as well as he could, but finally gave up, feeling he really hadn't succeeded in getting his point across. Pan American had several flights into Saigon, but he was told they were military charters reserved exclusively for service personnel.

"That's all we have," the ticket agent said, shrugging. "There's no way we can take civilians in there."

"Well, you'll need a crew, won't you?" Larry asked.

"Yes, but..."

Larry clicked his heels and stood tall. "Meet your new stewardess!"

The agent laughed, brought his fist down with an expletive and said, "It just might work." He reached out to shake Larry's hand. "If there's any way we can take you in, Dr. Ward, we'll do it."

Then, in order to have at least a pair of options, Larry rushed to Air Vietnam.

"I'd like to see the manager," he said to the girl at the front desk.

"I'm sorry, he's not here," she replied.

"Look," Larry insisted (a bit surprised at his own boldness), "I *know* he's here. I need to see him right now."

When the manager appeared, he told Larry what he had expected: "There's nothing scheduled until further notice."

"Well then, I want to charter a plane."

"We could charter you a plane, but you couldn't land," the manager explained.

"I'll take care of that. I'll get permission 'from the top' in Saigon."

The manager laughed. "Well, okay. Let's try. I'll get to work on the papers."

From there, Larry rushed to yet a third option, the office of a Bangkok travel service. He had learned of a man with a boat (perhaps a "gun runner") who somehow went in and out of Vietnam regularly. Larry let it be known that he wanted to be smuggled in on the next trip to Vietnam. He kept retracing his steps until he became known all over town as that desperate Yankee who *had* to get to Saigon. After Saigon, he was scheduled to visit Indonesia, so he had given his passport to the Indonesian Embassy in Bangkok.

Larry returned to his hotel room just in time to pick up the ringing phone. It was the man at the U.S. Embassy whom Larry had met at his first contact, but hadn't found particularly helpful. The man asked, "Do you have any kind of correspondent's accreditation?" Assured that Larry did indeed have such, the man said: "There's a special flight leaving this afternoon, taking in some news correspondents. If you can get there in twenty minutes, they should be able to put you on board."

"Great!" Larry responded and hung up. Only then did he remember: "Oh, no—my passport! It's at the Indonesian Embassy!"

He phoned Bert's room. "Get over to the Indonesian Embassy as fast as you can," he ordered. "Pound on the door if you have to. Get my passport and meet me at the Joint United States Military Advisory Group (JUSMAG). Be there in twenty minutes, not a second later."

Larry went to the JUSMAG offices, signed in, and finally boarded the bus that would take him to the airport, still watching for Bert. The bus was slowly pulling away when a taxi screeched to a stop. Bert popped out and ran alongside the bus. Larry calmly reached out the window, grabbed the precious documents, and saluted.

"All set!" he told the driver.

At the airport, it was discovered that Larry's smallpox vaccination had expired. Quickly, Captain William Robie of the U.S. military clinic at the airport, prepared a syringe, gave him the vaccination, and signed his World Health Organization yellow card, certifying that Larry was immunized. With a contingent of newsmen, Larry hurried onto the C-46 airplane, the engines already blaring. The airplane spun, aimed itself at the runway, lifted off, and set its course for Saigon.

As the plane began its descent for Tan Son Nhat Airport, the passengers could see the flares and the tracer bullets of war arching into the sky. Still, the plane landed safely. The passengers were told they would not be allowed to go into Saigon that night. They were taken to the officer's club, where everyone found accommodations.

When Larry reached the World Vision office the following morning, the horror of the battle that had ringed the office with death was on everyone's lips. Mel Van Peursem had watched the fighting from a window, despite the danger. Early in the morning, he had gotten into the World Vision Land Rover and cruised the streets, picking up bullet-ridden Vietnamese and carrying them to the hospital.

"Big Mel was an absolute hero," Larry recalled. "*Time* magazine carried a special item telling about some of his activities. Later, it was my very special privilege in the U.S. to present to him, at the request of the government of Vietnam, a medal that they awarded to Mel in gratitude for all he had done during the Tet crisis, even at the risk of his own life."

Getting from Saigon to Surabaya, Indonesia, again required the logistics of divine synergism. Larry kept praying, working, and watching. He knew commercial air service still had not been resumed in or out of Saigon but felt that somehow he should go out to the airport and try.

"There are no civilian flights out of Saigon," he was told at Tan Son Nhat. Larry was due in Singapore that night. He glanced out the window. "What about that new Air Vietnam 727 sitting out there on the runway?"

"Well, Air Vietnam has just taken delivery of it, but it can't stay here. They're taking it to Singapore."

"Singapore! When?"
"Today. Very soon."
"Can I go along?"
"If you have a ticket."
"Sell me one!"

Larry was the only passenger on board that plane on the short flight to Singapore. He had only the clothes on his back, a few U.S. dollars, and a credit card. In Singapore he checked into the Goodwood Park Hotel, bought an extra shirt, some underwear, a toothbrush, and some shaving cream. A morning flight took him to Surabaya. Business finished there, he hired a taxi for $35. The taxi carried him on the tedious, twenty-hour overland, dusty, hot journey through East Java back to Djakarta (now Jakarta), where he would catch a return flight to Saigon. But just as he arrived at the airport, he saw his plane taking off.

He checked his pockets: ten cents. He tried to find a hotel with an extra room, but there was none. No place to go. No money or food. Suddenly the whole situation struck him as quite funny. He described an incredible feeling of inner peace. "I was absolutely delighted to be on an adventure for God. I knew He was going to do something. Corrie ten Boom would have called it 'material for a miracle.'"

A stranger suddenly approached and said, "Pardon me, but aren't you Larry Ward? Are you having some problem? I'm a pastor here in town and I recognized you from a World Vision pastors' conference which I attended."

They shook hands vigorously.

"Where are you staying?" the pastor asked.

"Well, that's my problem," Larry ventured.

"No problem. You come and stay at our house."

At supper, the pastor introduced Larry to tremendous needs in Borneo, the first of a chain of events that would lead to World Vision's involvement in direct aid. Larry began to think; "Now I know why I missed that plane!" But there was more.

When the meal was finished, the pastor answered a knock at the front door.

"Dr. Ward, please come here a minute," the pastor called from the door.

At the door, Larry's mouth dropped open and he couldn't speak for a moment. The son of World Vision colleague David Morken exclaimed, "Larry Ward—I've been looking for you!" He had been dispatched to find Larry in connection with a projected series of World Vision sponsored meetings. He had looked for Larry nonstop since arriving in Djakarta. He was at the pastor's door only because the man he was with had stopped in on another matter.

God works in answer to prayer.

Ho Chi Minh died the following year. In 1970, the Indochina War became mired in even greater complexity. Just as in Larry's Civil War novel, *Thy Brother's Blood*, brother battled brother, and the South was no match for the ferocity and relentless determination of the forces from the North.

T. S. Eliot's poem, "The Waste Land," called April "the cruelest month, breeding lilacs out of the dead land, mixing memory and desire, stirring dull roots and spring rain."

For South Vietnam, it was the cruelest month indeed. Larry's *Living Light* for April 26, 1975, promised: "He is beloved of God and lives in safety beside Him. God surrounds him with His loving care, and preserves him from every harm. Let Him have all your worries and cares, for He is always thinking about you and watching everything that concerns you."

Larry would need it all. Streaming to the coastal cities in the sad "Convoy of Tears" came thousands of Vietnamese whose villages had been plundered. As a rescue plane in Nha Trang reached its capacity, throngs of people pressed through, desperate for a chance to escape. Somehow the door was forced shut, but people clung to the outside. The plane took off with refugees still holding onto the wings and wheels. When it landed in Saigon, the feet of dead Vietnamese could be seen hanging out the wheel wells where they had sought to hide. They had been crushed to death when the plane stowed its landing gear on takeoff.

Amid the fiercest battles, Larry continued his mission of service throughout South Vietnam. The village mentioned in the opening chapter of this book was Hiep Duc, on the morning after the Viet Cong had killed the district chief and his twelve-year-old daughter, leaving them hung on stakes. A small reconnaissance plane had spotted the grisly scene where 5,000 people had lost their homes in a burning inferno. Near the doorway of the command post, with the racket of war on all sides, Larry had looked down in the mud and found a Vietnamese New Testament opened to *Mac 16* (Mark 16). In the midst of war, some brother or sister in Christ had been reminded by the Scriptures that "he that believeth in me, though he were dead, yet shall he live."

The end of the Indochina war was near, but what was surely Larry Ward's greatest experience of service still lay ahead.

15

THE THREE

THROUGHOUT HIS LIFE, Larry carried one special, deeply personal concern for Vietnam. It began on the dark night of May 30, 1962, in the sleepy jungle town of Ban Me Thuot, Vietnam. Suddenly a cadre of barefoot Viet Cong soldiers shattered the stillness with machine gun fire. They raced to the Christian and Missionary Alliance's Leprosarium compound, tore open the doors, and ordered three missionaries to walk outside with their hands up. They rammed guns into their backs and led Dr. Eleanor Ardel Vietti, Archie Mitchell, and Mennonite volunteer Dan Gerber into the jungle, apparently never to be seen again. The American people abruptly were made to realize North Vietnam's designs on the South.

Larry had visited Ban Me Thuot on his first global journey and had formed a brief but close friendship with Dr. Vietti. Had the Viet Cong needed medical help for fighting troops? Was it a new wave of violence against foreigners? Was it a signal that all Christians were in danger? Shockwaves reverberated around the world. The Viet Cong, until this date, had advanced little more than threats.

As the years of the Indochina war ground on, the Christian church around the world prayed for the three missionaries' release. The hope of fellow believers, and later their resignation, was summed up by Archie Mitchell's thirteen-year-old daughter, Loretta, some three years after the kidnapping:

> *In everything give thanks. The Lord knows we love Daddy, but He wants Daddy for His work right now. Yes, "in everything give thanks." The only thing to do now is to stay and wait for the day when God's work through Daddy is finished, and then God will give Daddy back to us to enjoy.*

Burning in Larry Ward's heart was a quiet determination to pursue relentlessly every possibility for finding "the three" as he always referred to the early MIAs. He traveled in and out of Vietnam seventy-seven times during his years as Vice President/Overseas Director of World Vision and later as President of Food for the Hungry. With every visit, he carried the hope that this time he would stumble onto some clue that could lead to a resolution of this unfinished business and the release of these servants of Christ.

This hope led him time after time into the central highlands of Vietnam, where he suspected the missionaries and other U.S. prisoners of war might be held. Often a visit would yield some little clue, which he added to the rest, careful to keep a guarded silence about what was happening, out of concern for the families of the American missing.

The war ground on for thirteen more years. American families gave 56,000 of their sons in the vain attempt to hold back the North. The American combat forces had been withdrawn in 1972, yielding (in Larry's opinion) to domestic protests and media pressures rather than military reverses. American POWs in North Vietnam had been released in "Operation Homecoming" in January 1973. But Larry's friends—such as "the three" and Floyd Olson—were not among them.

With the direct American military presence withdrawn, the powerful forces from the North continued their war against the South, relentlessly pushing toward Saigon.

What about those missing missionaries and other Americans? Was there one last chance to get them out?

In November 1974, a tantalizing clue came from the Central Highlands where they had been captured. "Come and see," some

Montagnard contacts told Larry. "We have access to Americans still held in Vietnam."

Larry was skeptical. He knew it had been almost two full years since the American POWs held in North Vietnam had returned via "Operation Homecoming." He was also well aware of the long-standing desire for autonomy on the part of the Montagnards, who called themselves the Degar. This mountain tribe lived in the central highlands of Vietnam and was sometimes a despised ethnic minority to the Vietnamese majority. He told his friend, "If this is some ruse to get guns and money, forget it. It's just too late in history."

But the quiet insistence was, "They want you to come and see for yourself. But first they want you to carry this news to your president."

So Larry went to the president of the United States—or at least as close as he could get. President Gerald Ford was then in Japan, but through the help of one of Larry's closest friends, Winston Weaver, a World Vision board member and Mennonite church leader from Harrisonburg, Virginia, he secured an immediate appointment with John O. Marsh, then Chief of Staff in the White House (and later the Secretary of the Army).

After a brief but encouraging conference with Mr. March, whose courtesy Larry remembered with the deepest appreciation, there was a busy whirl of meetings in the White House. Larry was assigned Dr. Ted Marrs (actually General Marrs, a retired Air Force medical leader) to be his principal contact.

It should be explained that certain elements of this story were always required to be kept secret, for the safety of those people remaining in Vietnam. Essentially, the situation in Vietnam had developed out of the zeal of Christian Montagnards in South Vietnam in sharing the Gospel with their fellow tribe members who were serving on the side of the North. Warm ties of friendship had developed. The idea of "why do we fight other people's wars; why don't we get together?" had prevailed, and a special alliance had developed. This group, which was seeking American support, realized that one of the best ways to get this was to be able to prove the existence of Americans still missing in action in their highlands.

The events of the month that followed, from November 1974 until late April 1975, could well be the subject of another book. It had been suggested that they could even make the ingredients of an outstanding and successful Hollywood movie or TV presentation. They read like fiction, but they were all true. (Larry would later add, "Sadly true.")

In the weeks that followed the November contact, Larry made several trips to Vietnam. He was there almost constantly from late January until the dying days of South Vietnam in late April. High up in the hills of central Vietnam, he met with his Montagnard friends, and with their contacts from among what they called "the tribes in the jungle," those who had been recruited by the Viet Cong or North Vietnam.

Larry remembered the unusual experience of personally typing a document ("poignantly historic," he called it), which set forth the hopes of the Montagnards. It was a unique "Declaration of Peace." It was their hope that their friend Larry Ward might read this for them on the floor of the United Nations, or arrange for some world leader to do so.

Larry recalled, "It was interesting how this developed. They were talking in a polyglot of tribal languages, Vietnamese, French, and for my benefit, such English as they could muster. Then there would be a slow, laborious translation from one tribal language into another, and then into English for me and then I would type it."

Larry kept a copy of that document. It said in effect that the tribe's people were tired of fighting someone else's war. They were ready to lay down their arms, except in defense of their own homes and families. It was especially meaningful to Larry, because the whole basis of communication between these groups had been the sharing of the message of Jesus Christ. Now, as brothers in Christ, they were trying to unite in a plea to the outside world to help them.

Part of the plan was for Larry to visit the battle areas near Ban Me Thuot to see at least a few of the American prisoners and to receive evidence of others. But there were problems.

The original high-ranking officer he was to meet (who had become a Christian and was open to this contact) was recalled to Hanoi. Another man took his place and for some weeks, it was uncertain as to whether or not this new man could be trusted.

But finally, on March 6, 1975, Larry was handed a cryptic note in Saigon. It said simply, "The Committee accepts the presence of the foreigner on the Committee. April 1."

This meant that at long last he was to meet with these people in the jungle and if they did exist, to see some of the captured Americans. His heart was beating fast as he boarded a flight for the United States. He stopped briefly at home and then flew quickly across the United States to meet in the Pentagon with Dr. Robert Shields in the Department of Defense, the very man who had coordinated Operation Homecoming and was now in charge of the continuing search for the missing Americans.

Larry had barely arrived in Washington when a telephone call from Saigon brought startling news. Ban Me Thuot had fallen. Within a few hours, this was followed by the announcement that President Thieu had withdrawn all his troops from the hills.

Larry's mission seemed doomed to failure. His rendezvous would be cancelled, for there was apparently no way to keep that meeting in the jungle.

He returned to Saigon anyway, arriving one night and immediately flying the next morning to Dalat. It was a strange experience for Larry, for he and his young Montagnard friend, Ha Johnny (son of the famed Sao A) were the only passengers on the plane going to Dalat. The exodus was on, and everyone else was headed south while these two flew north on their mission of mercy.

"The next few days in Dalat were strange," Larry summarized. "The missionaries had all fled in response to a warning that the Viet Cong or Northern Vietnamese were on their way. They can be forgiven for their sudden flight, for they knew that a number of their fellow missionaries had been captured in Ban Me Thuot."

In Dalat, Larry and Johnny's brother Ha Jimmy had a long series of meetings with "a motley group" of tribal leaders. The developments in the Central Highlands had produced some strange bedfellows. While Larry and the others met inside, Montagnard Viet Cong troops provided security outside.

A prime question in these discussions was how Larry, as an American, could make his way over the mountains into Ban Me

Thuot, to keep that long-postponed meeting. He would have been willing to try the long hike, but to do so would have endangered his companions. He was the last American left in the Central Highlands to anyone's knowledge, and there was no way he could have disguised himself effectively.

Finally, a plan was established. If Larry and Ha Jimmy could fly over a rendezvous point in the jungles, the old "Camp Zulu" Special Forces Camp, friendly tribespeople on the ground would radio to them whether or not it was safe for them to land in Ban Me Thuot, even though it was in Communist hands.

The problem was to get that plane.

Through a miraculous circumstance (described in Chapter 15 of this book), Larry was able to fly with Jimmy south to Saigon on what was probably the last flight to leave Dalat. The city fell that night, as one of the "dominoes" toppling across central and northern South Vietnam.

Back in Saigon, Larry resolutely set out in search of that airplane. Dr. Marrs, from the White House, had given him the name of Colonel John Madison of the Joint Four-Party Military Team, the man who was in communication with the North Vietnamese and Laotian authorities about the missing Americans and other humanitarian issues.

Larry summarized the plan to Colonel Madison. "We need a light plane to fly over the Central Highlands. The Montagnards will be on the ground with a radio at 'Camp Zulu' in the Highlands, and we will receive instructions from them as to whether or not we can land at Ban Me Thuot."

Colonel Madison leaned back in his chair and reflected. He seemed helpful, but there was no hope in his speech. "Can you get to the Vietnamese?"

Of course Larry could get to the Vietnamese, but he felt the Colonel was missing the point. This new movement, the United Montagnard Front (UMF), would be a move against *all Vietnamese*. Their "wall of peace" would be a barrier against the Vietnamese of both North and South. Five months earlier, the Montagnard who had carried this message to Saigon had disappeared. He was believed to be dead. Larry's Montagnard friends were convinced that U.S.

Embassy personnel had thoughtlessly relayed the Montagnards' report to the South Vietnamese, not understanding or thinking through all of the implications. They were almost certain the South Vietnamese had done him in.

Despite all that happened, Larry now had no choice but to take his plea to the South Vietnamese. They might, he reasoned, see the UMF as an ally and at this late hour enter into the mission to keep their country free. All this was taking place at a time when missionaries in other countries were suspected of being agents of the U.S. Central Intelligence Agency. Was Larry?

"I am not employed by the CIA, and never was. While I am not a pacifist and while I still feel there are causes (such as freedom) worth fighting for and dying for, I long ago have learned as a Christian to hate war. My work had taken me into just too many battlefields; my hands have been stained with dying blood too many times. War cannot be God's first choice for the people of his creation."

But now, there was no choice. With the possibility that the lives of Americans missing in action were at stake, he was prepared to go to the Vietnamese with his plea. If they don't care about the missing Americans, at least they might be interested in the potential military resource of some 200,000 united Montagnards who were ready and probably able to retake Ban Me Thuot and Pleiku and Dalat. Even at this late date, they might feel there was a chance to reverse the "domino" movement South Vietnam was experiencing. Lives were at stake. Haste was important. Larry would go to the Vietnamese.

As he walked out of Colonel Madison's office he noticed that the halls of the DAO were lined with boxes packed for shipment home. One box in particular caught Larry's eye. It was addressed to Col. John Madison, at an address in Arlington, Virginia. "Colonel Madison was a good man," Larry reflected, "But the total mentality in those hours was exodus." Evacuation was in the air. What chance was there to carry out his plan?

Larry went to colonels and generals and cabinet officials of the South Vietnamese, contacting this person and that, working his way up to General Cao Hao Hun in the office of the Prime Minister, to his friend General Le Nguyen Khang, Deputy Chief of the Joint Chiefs of Staff, and to many others of high rank.

What happened? Larry typically would pour out his heart to a high official for over a half hour. He would tell the whole story of the missing Americans and the uniting Montagnards and present his need for just one little airplane to make a single pass over the jungle.

One official listened intently. Larry knew this particular Vietnamese man spoke good English and had understood every word. He leaned forward, waiting for helpful suggestions that he hoped would come from the man's expertise and authority. Instead the officer said earnestly, "My wife and I want to get out of here. Can you help us?"

Larry mumbled something and quickly left. Of course he would help the man if he could, but all in good time. At this moment, all he could think about was the haunting refrain: "We have seventy to eighty Americans." Possibly among them were "The Three" for whom the world of Christendom had prayed and for whom he had searched so long. He had stood up for Howard Newton at Norwich High when a teacher made a fool out of his classmate; now he would stand up for those in 1975 who could not rescue themselves.

From all of his meetings came one noteworthy contact. His good friend General Nguyen Van Chuc, now Deputy Minister for Refugee Resettlement, suggested that Larry meet with President Nguyen Van Thieu.

Larry would explain, "I had met with him a number of times at the palace and had been a dinner guest in Thieu's home. But I knew that getting to him now would not be easy. Other high-ranking people who had proposed that I see the president had told me frankly that they didn't know how it could be arranged."

By now, it was April 20, 1975. Hopefully, the friends in the jungle waited. President Thieu remained absolutely inaccessible, blockaded by his own staff for reasons still not clear. Larry needed an excuse to enter the palace and make his plea.

But then Larry's old friend Bob Pierce arrived in Saigon and he had his answer. Bob would be his ticket. The plan would be to arrange an appointment for Bob with Madame Thieu, the president's wife. Ordinarily, Larry would have called her to make an appointment for himself, but he had just met with her a few days earlier to discuss a joint refugee relief project with her ladies' committee. He needed a fresh excuse.

Larry told his friend, "Bob, you are that excuse. All I want to do is to get inside the palace and tell Madame Thieu that I *must* see her husband."

The meeting was memorable. After Madame Theiu warmly welcomed them, Dr. Pierce came quickly to the point. "Madame Thieu, you know I'm glad to see you. But that's not why we are here. Larry *must* see your husband. It is a matter of the utmost importance."

She sprang to her feet, "I'll go get him."

Larry stood quickly, pleased but a bit startled. "We didn't mean *now*," he said apologetically. "We thought perhaps you could make an appointment."

Madame Thieu shook her head, "I'll go get him," she said rather firmly, and quickly left the room.

A moment later, the president himself appeared in the doorway. Without a word, Madame Thieu and the ladies of her committee left the room before Larry could thank her.

For the next forty-five minutes, while Bob Pierce sat nearby praying silently, Larry poured out his story, starting from the beginning.

"Mr. President," he concluded, "you know that all these years we have never asked you for anything. We have just come, so many times, to offer our help. But this time, without apology, I *ask* you for something. I need an airplane. I need to fly over the jungles, to make the contact I have just told you about.

"Perhaps I have no reason to ask you to care about American lives as this point. I know you are bitter about the withdrawal of American support. I can understand your attitude. But on behalf of the parents in America who gave 56,000 of their sons to die for this country and on behalf of the parents whose sons are still missing in action, for their sakes and out of respect for their sacrifice, I *plead* with you now to help me."

Larry had fought to hold his emotions in check as he talked. Now it wasn't so easy, for the president's own luminous eyes were suddenly glistened.

Larry pressed on. "I do not ask you, sir, to risk any Vietnamese lives. All I need is an airplane. We will fly it ourselves. If you can't give me one, please sell me one. If I can't buy one, I may steal one. I *must* fly over the spot, I must, sir. Before I die, I must know if any of this is true, if in fact there are American prisoners still alive out there."

President Thieu looked straight at Larry, his eyes now full of tears.

"Mr. President, there was a day in our country when the youth of America wore black armbands to protest the war. I understood their questions and confusion, but you may remember the cable I sent you on that day. It said, 'When the last American has left Vietnam, I will gladly come back and stand beside you and die with you, because of my great love for Vietnam.'"

Larry was too moved to say more, except one choked word: "Please."

Nguyen Van Thieu leaned back, holding out his hands, palms up. "What have we to lose?" He smiled through his own tears, "What have we to lose?"

Suddenly, Larry was aware of a presence in the doorway, even though he kept his eyes glued to the president's face. Thieu looked at his watch then jumped to his feet, "Oh, I am late for a meeting," he said. "I am late. I will call you."

For the first time, Bob Pierce spoke in a strangely soft and gentle voice. "Mr. President, Larry and I would like to pray for you."

"Of course," said the president. "Of course."

While the dignitaries waited in the next room for their meeting (apparently the one at which President Theiu would be "persuaded" to resign), three men stood close together in the palace and bowed their heads. The president reached out to put one arm around Larry, the other around Bob Pierce, as Bob prayed simply and to the point: "Father, help this man to do what is best for his country, whatever it costs him personally. In Jesus' name, Amen."

And the President softly echoed, "Amen."

Larry turned to the president, who took his right hand in both of his. With a face wet with tears he opened his mouth as if to speak, then bit his lip and shook his head, too full for words. He turned and left the room.

Several hours passed before Larry saw him again. As he entered the hotel where he was staying, Larry saw the president on television, announcing his resignation, bitterly lamenting the failure of the Americans to help South Vietnam in this, its last crisis hour of need.

Larry listened, sagged, and then went to his room and knelt beside his bed: "Father, I really don't understand this. I thought you had led me into all this. The president seemed to be our last hope."

But God's synchrony was right on time. Another drum was rolling in the distance. He had miles to go before he slept.

16

LET MY PEOPLE GO!

IT SEEMS THAT all of Larry Ward's life had been an example of God's synchrony: the smooth blending of events to accomplish the Lord's purposes. Nowhere was this more evident than in those incredible last days in South Vietnam, in 1975.

To highlight just a few of the incredible people that fit into what Larry once unhesitatingly described as "the greatest experience of all my life," consider these three scenes and what they later represented.

Scene No. 1:

Larry sat on the Vietnam Airlines plane with his papers spread out before him, as usual making his airplane seat his "office." But now, the papers lie untouched, as he talked with an earnest young Vietnamese flight attendant. It was March 6, 1975 and the dominoes had not yet begun to fall in Vietnam. But this young flight attendant was something of a prophet. He was earnestly predicating to Larry that the fall of South Vietnam was not too long in the distance. By the time the flight landed in Hong Kong, all that Larry could do was gather up his papers with a strange sense of God's leading. "I didn't get my work done, but somehow my heart tells me that there was something very important about this contact. Perhaps in God's own time I will see what it was."

Scene No. 2:

Later that same day, on the continuing flight from Tokyo to the United States, Larry unexpectedly encountered his old Vietnamese associate, Dr. Garth Hunt. Now Director of Living Bibles International in Canada, Garth listened with great interest as Larry reported the continuing chain of events in Vietnam. He and his associates, Dr. Jacob Bellig and Dr. W. Brooks, plied Larry with questions. When the flight landed, Larry deplaned with the strange and lingering sense of special significance related to this conversation.

Scene No. 3:

Flying this time *into* Vietnam, Larry was in an interesting conversation with a somewhat mysterious U.S. government person. The man said that he held (or at least had held) the rank of captain, but he was nonspecific about his responsibilities. The two developed a quick rapport, Larry enjoyed the conversation and yet, again, his heart somehow told him that the significance of the conversation lay beyond that day.

Why these scenes? What do they represent? Consider these developments:

Scene No. 1 Flashback:

Over a month later, Larry and his companion Ha Jimmy found themselves in a scene of incredible confusion, "almost chaos," in the airport in Dalat, high up in the Central Highlands in Vietnam. To Larry's knowledge, he was the last American in those hills. The rush was on, the wild flight to the South. Larry and Ha Jimmy believed they *must* get to Saigon. There were important developments related to his long-standing concerns about those American missing in action. But there were no seats on the plane and the wild crowd, jostling and almost fighting for seats, waving fistfuls of U.S. dollars, didn't even permit him to reach the counter. Being an American, at this late date in Vietnam's history, was of no advantage. Suddenly,

Larry felt a hand on his arm. He turned to face the same flight attendant he had met on the flight from Saigon to Hong Kong.

"Some problem?"

Larry nodded. "I need two seats to Saigon."

"Don't talk," the flight attendant said crisply. "Meet me inside." Inside he handed Larry two tickets and within a matter of minutes Larry and Jimmy were airborne, headed from Dalat. What they did not know was that Dalat would fall that night. On board the plane, Larry chatted with the flight attendant.

The young main said, "I know you understand, sir, why I couldn't talk with you there. Everyone wants to get out."

"Of course," Larry replied. "Do you come to Dalat often?"

The man looked at him strangely. "You remember me. I met you on the flight from Saigon to Hong Kong. I am an *international* steward. This is *the only time in my life* I ever come to Dalat!"

Looking back on that scene, Larry explained: "Humanly speaking, I owe my life to that young man. He was in exactly the right spot at the right time to help Jimmy and me—and I know God had his hand in this."

Scene No. 2 Flashback

April 25, 1975. Larry once again was in a scene of noise and confusion, at the Tan Son Nhat Airport. This was the U.S. military's command center for organizing the escape from Vietnam for people who needed get out. With Larry was a small group of friends (the vanguard of the many hundreds he was to help in the next few hours). They *must* get out of Vietnam. These were people who had distinguished themselves in the service of their country. They had links with the U.S. government, just by virtue of that country's presence in their land.

Larry looked around uncertainly, not knowing just how to start or what to do. Suddenly he looked across the room. Standing there was Dr. Garth Hunt.

Larry often said, "One of the greatest tributes I could pay to Garth Hunt is that somehow I was not the least bit surprised to see him there in Vietnam. He had been away for over three years. He had no reason to be there. I found out later that he had promised his wife Betty as he left for Asia that this was one place he would not go, back into the dangers of Vietnam."

However, Garth Hunt's heart, the constraining love of Christ, had drawn him back to that country where he and Betty had served so long and faithfully. Friends of his were in trouble, and he was determined to help. Also, he knew that there in Saigon was the unfinished manuscript to the new Vietnamese New Testament, the first such translation in readable language that the Vietnamese people had for many years. He was determined to get that manuscript and bring it out, along with any of his friends he could help. But as a Canadian, it would be very difficult for him to sponsor anyone in the midst of this frantic exodus.

Now there was a quick look of recognition on his part, and then the two quickly went to work. Garth had been there long enough to size up the situation. He directed Larry to the desks in the command center where U.S. civilians were presenting their case for Vietnamese friends they wanted to help out of the country.

Scene No. 3 Flashback:

Larry shrugged, selected one of the lines at random, and looked in astonishment at the man behind the desk. It was that same mysterious person with whom he had flown into Saigon. There was a flicker of recognition, but no direct communication. Larry understood, and when his turn came, he quietly stepped up to represent his case. The man told him what to do and handed him the necessary forms. As Larry walked away, he realized that in those papers, he had the key to unlock the door to freedom for unknown numbers of his friends.

A moment later he saw the man behind the desk enjoying a cup of coffee during a little break. Larry slipped over beside him. "I know you understand why I couldn't especially greet you," the man said. "Everybody has a case to present here."

Larry assured him he understood—and then asked, "Is this the procedure we follow? I have many others I want to help."

Assured that it was the correct procedure, Larry breathed a word of thanks and walked into the middle of one of his life's greatest service experiences. All told, he and Garth were able to help over 1,800 people find a new life of freedom in other parts of the world.

Together, Garth and Larry went to work. In addition to those who were now already on their way to the United States or elsewhere abroad through their efforts and Larry's specific sponsorship, there were many others to be helped.

In the hours that followed, they fanned out all over the city, contacting these people, going again and again to the airport. One of Garth's contacts was with a beloved friend who for years had been the leader of the Protestant Evangelical Church in Vietnam. "Sir," Garth pleaded, "you must come with me. You have been in America. You have been known as the friend of the Americans, at least the American missionaries. Please come."

The servant of God smiled gently. "Thank you, Mr. Hunt, but as the president of the church, I am like the captain of the ship. I should be the *last* to leave. Not all of our pastors will be able to go. I'm grateful for those you can help, but I will stay. Just pray for me that I do not fail my test."

As the hours ticked by, it became increasingly difficult to reenter the airport. Larry and Garth never knew for certain whether they themselves would be permitted through the gates or if they would be able to bring anymore of their Vietnamese friends along. They had, however, an important group of about seventy key people whom they had asked to meet them on a certain corner in the city of Saigon. The big question was to figure out how to get them past the Vietnamese guards and then past the American guards and on board the planes that would carry them to safety.

Probably not even realizing the unusual importance of what they were doing, the two agreed to charter a city bus. Loaded with its precious cargo of men and women, boys and girls, it approached the gates of Tan Son Nhat Airport. It must have presented an odd spectacle. Leaning out one window was Garth Hunt, barking away in his fluent Vietnamese.

Leaning out of the other side was Larry Ward, waving a sheaf of papers that bore the red corporate seal of Food for the Hungry/Vietnam. Up ahead was a car driven by an American working with the United States Agency for International Development (USAID). He was holding a radio in his hand, periodically talking into the radio and then pointing back over his shoulders to the bus behind. Larry, meanwhile, was holding a similar small radio, and pointing earnestly at the white car preceding them. No matter that both of those radios were dead. They were all part of a very convincing, confusing, and therefore effective approach.

The guards could handle those generals in the jeeps and those big Mercedes cars. They just didn't know what to do with the bus or with these two foreigners talking all at once in a mixture of rapid-fire Vietnamese and English. The gates rolled open, and the bus entered.

The events that followed were miracles of God's timing.

Larry had gone so many times to the desk to present his case that finally someone handed him a whole sheaf of airplane manifest forms. "No point in duplicating our work, mister," someone said. "Just fill these out and bring them in."

In Larry's hands were the papers that could bring literally thousands of Vietnamese, many of whom he knew personally, to safety. He would unhesitatingly vouch for them and without hesitation sign his name to the papers assuming all responsibilities for their future conduct in the United States.

Time and again, one of those sheets of paper would have a certain number or spaces to be filled out. For example, there might be five spaces and just at that moment a mother and father would appear with their three young children. By the time that Larry and Garth themselves finally boarded the flight that was to carry their last group on its way, every single person with whom they had been able to establish direct contact had been put on those manifests. The list had come out exactly right.

There was a scene at the gate that Larry would never forget. Assisting him and Garth was a remarkable lady, Madam Nguyen Ngoc Le, President of the Vietnam War Widows Association. The widow of a famous general and former head of the Vietnamese Red Cross, she had been one of the most outstanding Vietnamese helping her people through the years.

Today, she herself was a general. As Garth and Larry brought their various groups up to the actual place where they would go through the final gate to board the planes, she was there barking out orders in Vietnamese. "Stand straight," she would say, "Be proud. Leave your country with your head high."

When Garth had led the last group through the gate and only Madam Le and her friend Larry remained, she looked at him and wilted. Placing her head on his shoulder, she sobbed over and over again: "Now those terrible men will destroy my beautiful country!"

It was as if she herself, in leaving, somehow felt that this was the ultimate surrender. Larry placed a gentle arm around her shoulder and supported her as they boarded, and then with the rest of the refugees, sat down on the floor of the plane to be lifted from the scene of confusion below.

That night, the airport was rocketed. The first forces of the Viet Cong and the North Vietnamese spilled in. All flights were suspended. Anyone else leaving would have to be evacuated by helicopter.

Larry and his friends flew to Clark Field in Manila, and what Larry insisted on calling "the miracles" continued. For example, there were three groups about which he felt a special concern: the one that he and Garth had accompanied and two others. But they did not know where the other two were. Perhaps they had flown directly to Guam, or even to the United States.

Larry was anxious to keep his group together. Already, flying from Saigon to Manila, he and Garth had mapped out the concept that was going to result in the formation of "Hope Village" in the United States. He wasn't just going to dump all those Vietnamese refugees on the American economy. He was going to set up a job placement and general orientation program to help them really succeed.

They had helped him, and others like him, in their own country. He was determined to help them. But how and where would he go about finding those two groups in particular, and then the many others he had signed out of Vietnam?

The answer was not long in coming. Larry and Garth and their group had arrived late at night at Clark Field. The next morning, along with thousands of other refugees, they were being bused to the processing centers at Clark Field.

As their bus neared one corner, a four-way stop, Larry shouted out. "Garth, look! There's one of our groups!"

Shouting to his driver to wait, Larry leaped out of the bus and raced into the center of the intersection, waving frantically at the other bus. Out of that bus came one of his Vietnamese friends, and they fell into each other's arms. But, suddenly they turned as they heard another shout. From another corner came a tall Vietnamese friend, the leader of the third group. He reached out and threw his arms around Larry in a big bear hug.

Providentially, those three groups had arrived at that very intersection at the same moment.

There was a quick conversation. "Where are you staying? What section?"

Arrangements were made. Within hours, these three groups and about 150 other people were on the next leg of their journey toward Guam.

At Andersen Field in Guam (now called Andersen Air Force Base), it seemed that they had run into a snag. Larry had earnestly pleaded with the authorities to allow him to take his entire group to the United States together. He already had the "Hope Village" concept in mind. With him were the 241 who had flown from Clark Field to Guam and now others had joined their number, so he and Garth had about 360 or more in their custody.

The young lieutenant who was in charge of the program listened sympathetically, but finally shook his head. "Sorry," he said. "I don't think I can help you. This is all computerized. There are no groups. The people just go by individual families, as their numbers are called." Larry and his little band stepped aside and looked at each other. In Guam, he and Garth had been joined by missionary John Newman, his old friend from Dalat, who had left Vietnam some weeks before the fall; Reverend John Sawin, veteran Christian and Missionary Alliance missionary; and Larry's good friend Drew Sawin, John's son.

"Let's call the White House," someone said. "Let's call Billy Graham! (Drew had informed the group that he was aware that the White house was indeed monitoring the progress of this group around the world, and that he had been informed that Billy Graham was going to have breakfast with President Ford).

Larry shook his head. "Guys," he said quietly, "the Lord himself has brought us this far. We have seen his miracles. Let's just trust him."

About fifteen minutes later, that young lieutenant burst into their barracks. "Can you get your group together?"

Larry smiled. "They're all right here. We have already called them together."

"Well," the lieutenant said, "we don't understand it, but a 747 has just come in which somehow was missed on the schedule. It's all yours if you want it! It will take your whole group, and a few more."

A few days later, as the refugees were being loaded into the buses that would carry them to their plane, Larry stepped over to thank the lieutenant. "Aw," the man insisted, "I was just doing my job."

"No," said Larry gratefully. "You have done more, and we'll be forever grateful."

The lieutenant looked at Larry for a long moment and then said quietly, "I was a prisoner in North Vietnam. I just had to help."

Larry would often say that it seemed that all along the line, God had the right people at the right place at the right moment to help. These were people whose hearts had been touched in some special way.

As they boarded the Pan Am jet, Garth and Larry stepped up to the helpful flight attendant. "We would like to give some instructions to them in Vietnamese, and then, if it's all right with you, we would like to have a special prayer." She readily agreed, and a moment later Garth's rapid fire Vietnamese crackled over the plane sound system. Then he brought to the microphone an aged patriarch of the church, Pastor Le Van Thai, to lead in prayer.

"I will never forget that prayer." Larry recalled. "I can't have a dry eye as I recall those words. Pastor Le Van Thai not only thanked God for their deliverance, but prayed especially for the church left behind, for their brothers and sisters and friends, and for all of their country, in the hours of trial that would follow."

And then that big bird stretched what Larry always called "its happy wings" and mounted into the sky. As the plane flew toward the United States, in the quiet of the night, Larry silently walked from one end to the other. His heart was full of praise to God. He looked down on his sleeping Vietnamese friends, many of whom he had known so well through the years. "I felt like the last chapter of a Grace Livingston Hill book," he would recount with a chuckle, "with all the characters assembled in the last chapter. Here they were, relaxed and happy—on their way to freedom."

And then, leaning back to relax, he remembered that night in early April when it had become apparent to him that the forces of the North were going to prevail. He thought of all those with whom his life had been linked in service through the years. He remembered those who had been approaching him everywhere he went asking him if he could help them get out.

And, reflecting on the airplane en route to the United States, he remembered that particular day when all of this had burdened his heart so that he had fallen on his knees in prayer in his hotel room. He had been praying for this one and that one, and for all of troubled Vietnam. Suddenly his prayer had reached such intensity that he found himself on his feet, holding up his hands to God and crying out: "Let my people go!"

That had been his cry. He had cried out, and the Lord had heard him.

17

"PROJECT NOAH"

THEY CALLED IT "Project Noah," and Larry Ward always regarded it as one of his life's greatest experiences.

But, he also would admit it came to a rather untimely and inglorious end.

"Project Noah" was one of the first efforts (very likely *the* first) of Vietnamese refugee "boat people" to escape from their war-shattered homeland.

The project had an unusual cast of characters: the indefatigable Larry Ward, the peripatetic Dr. Bob Pierce, miscellaneous high-level Vietnamese (disguised as homeless refugees), a lovable old Navy man named Bill Pride (whom Larry described as "more by nature than most of us are by grace"), and a colorful and much-decorated Air Force hero, Colonel Jack Bailey (whom Larry simply and sincerely labeled "the most genuinely compassionate person I have ever met").

The "scenes" rival the cast: secret meetings, code names (Larry's was "Gray Eagle"), a mysterious cache in Larry's hotel room (complete with smoke grenades, an unloaded machine gun, and even an American flag!), and a wild chase through Saigon streets, with gunfire shattering the curfew quiet.

In one exciting episode, Larry's hotel room was jammed with Vietnamese (perhaps twenty or thirty) waiting for the signal to rush to the docks for their escape from Vietnam on two small ships. It had been decided that Larry should stay on to handle any problems that might arise with the Vietnamese government. Jack Bailey would accompany these first boat people, who would head for the Philippines as soon as they reached the open sea.

Bill Pride, the old Navy hand, had flown to Manila to make arrangements with the government there. Because these were the first of the boat people, no one knew how President Marcos might react. (Larry had planned Project Noah originally to help fourteen Vietnamese staff of the Far East Broadcasting Company [FEBC] in their escape from Vietnam, and so now he had sent Bill Pride to FEBC in Manila.)

Telephone and telegraph facilities were almost non-existent in these dying hours of South Vietnam. Anyway, this was a highly secret mission. Larry had devised a code. FEBC news broadcasts could be picked up in Saigon, and so he sent word via Bill Pride to Newscaster Carl Lawrence to give a coded message on the morning news.

Larry would never forget that day and that electric moment when Carl flashed the word: "That concludes the news," he said. "And now, here's a thought for the day. Take *pride* in your lawn."

That was the first signal! Bill Pride had made contact. But what would come next? If Carl continued, "make your neighbors *red* with envy," that would signal a delay or a problem.

"Take pride in your lawn," stated Carl Lawrence in Manila. "Make your neighbors *green* with envy!"

Larry leaped to his feet. "It's a go. Scramble!"

His group rushed out of the hotel, raced to waiting cars and hurried toward the docks. All over Saigon, others switched off their radios and scrambled.

Suffice it to say that Project Noah hit a premature Ararat when the 132 refugees and Colonel Jack Bailey were stopped by crooked elements of the South Vietnamese police four hours down the Saigon River. It was not a legal arrest. It was kidnap and ransom, with the entire party held for days in a dirty warehouse on the riverfront. When an angry Larry tracked them down, first of all demanding the release of the American, Bailey was rushed away in a jeep, perhaps to be disposed of. Knowing that Larry was running behind the jeep, Jack attempted to escape. That's when the shots rang out.

Unfortunately, Jack leaped from the jeep in front of a jail, and was immediately captured and dragged inside.

Jack suffered for over a week in that jail, actually in a "dungeon underneath the jail," as he would explain. He was threatened, beaten, tortured—and even given truth serum in an attempt to find out whom the mysterious Larry Ward was and where he could be located.

On the advice of high-level Vietnamese friends, Larry himself finally went into hiding, first in an empty apartment, and then in a hotel under an assumed name.

After a long week, Jack's release was finally obtained by direct presidential order after some of Larry's Vietnamese friends had intervened.

"Jack still bears both the physical and psychological scars of that ordeal," Larry summarized. "But he has kept on helping, first in our 1975 Hope Village operation for Indochina refugees and later when he launched his own mercy ship operation in the South China Sea." Food for the Hungry donated its *S.S. Akuna* to Jack's program in 1982.

*

18

HIS BROTHER'S KEEPER

SOUTH VIETNAM fell on April 30, 1975, ending a thirty-year carnage for the Vietnamese people and putting an end to the American nightmare which had taken the lives of 56,000 soldiers. Larry's exodus from Vietnam (in which he was able to take with him some 1,800 people who might have been killed or imprisoned by the invaders) was described in the preceding chapter.

"I am certain," he told his associates back in the United States, "that Vietnamese now are going to pour into Thailand by the thousands. Let's get in there and see what we can do right away to prepare for them."

That foresight allowed Food for the Hungry to be one of the first humanitarian agencies from outside to be ready with aid to these homeless people.

On his first tour of a camp in northern Thailand, Larry noticed a young Hmong tribesman following him as he inspected the facilities. His eyes were bright, his countenance sad. When he got the chance he whispered to Larry in perfect English, "Sir, it is true. We do have food and we do have place to sleep. But, sir, we have no hope."

"No hope." The words stung. The people had fled with nothing, but that is not what caused them the worst suffering. It was a lack of hope for the future. Before Larry stepped into the khaki-colored Thai government helicopter to leave, he looked up into the sky. "Lord," he prayed, "there is always hope with You. But what hope can You provide for these people?"

Sleep came hard that night because the face of the Hmong intruded his mind, and he heard over and over the words, "no hope." The Hmong are ambitious and bright people. This young man who could speak English had probably worked in some capacity for the U.S. government.

The following day brought a call from Lionel Rosenblatt, chief of U.S. refugee operations in Thailand. Larry described Lionel as "a real hero in South Vietnam's last days, and an outstanding foreign service officer". Rosenblatt had seen Food for the Hungry's Hope Village in California and now wanted to discuss with Larry some matters concerning the refugees in Thailand.

They met in the coffee shop of the Asia Hotel in Bangkok where Rosenblatt introduced Dr. Yang Dao, one of the educated exceptions among the basically illiterate Hmong refugees. He had earned a Ph.D. in France, had served as a high official in the government of Laos before leaving as a refugee, and was now concerned about the future of his people.

"Dr. Ward," he said, "I know that you want to help my people. But please remember, we are a people in need of development. Please do not take us to your country or to Canada, or to France, or to Australia. We will not fit in."

Then he added a line that somehow made the light go on: "Somewhere in the world there must be a developing country where we can go and develop with it and even contribute to its development."

Larry looked at Dr. Yang Dao and said, "Thank you." Then he looked straight up and breathed a quick prayer, "And thank *you*, God."

After the meeting, he rushed back to his room and said to his wife, "Lorraine, honey, we have a job to do. He rubbed his hands together vigorously, with his lips pinched tightly shut. "We've got to scour this earth. God has given us the formula for helping these people find a future and a hope. Not just to come to America where they really won't fit in, but to relocate in some developing country which needs people like them."

The trail led first to the welcome arms of Nicaragua, where permission actually was obtained to bring in a pilot group of 15,000 Vietnamese refugees. But, Larry and his associates quickly backed off when they sensed the human rights issues involved and felt that the refugees would have been placed in a very dangerous situation.

But the experience of studying the situation in Nicaragua had led to a clear understanding of what could be accomplished by "resettlement through development" or, perhaps more correctly, "development through resettlement."

Larry explained, "We are grateful for the learning experience of the negotiations with Nicaragua and the Somoza Government. They had about two percent of their people living in forty-seven percent of their landmass in the Atlantic Zone. It could have been an ideal situation for the refugees, except that we could see the war clouds on the horizon. But, we did grow all the more reinforced in our conviction that here was a solid answer to the refugee resettlement problem in the world. The secret would be to take people not just where they would be accepted on humanitarian grounds, but where they would be welcome because they were *needed*."

There were other contacts—with Argentina and with Paraguay, for example, but concern for the refugees and their best interests seemed to indicate that these would not be the best situations.

And then came Bolivia, and in Larry's words, "one of the strangest experiences of all my life."

Bolivia was the ideal example of a country that needed people, especially jungle farmers such as the refugees. In early 1978, arrangements were completed to bring in a pilot group of 100 families. On the surface, it seemed ideal. Each family would receive 120 acres of land for free. They would have full citizenship rights after one year, upon application. And Food for the Hungry, as the coordinating agency, would be there to assure that their human rights were protected.

In April 1978, Larry signed the official agreement with the Ministry of Foreign Affairs of the government of Bolivia. This was done in the presence of two Hmong refugees who had been flown to Bolivia to survey the situation for themselves.

The refugees returned to their fellows in Thailand, like the two in the Bible who had gone to "spy out the land." They reported enthusiastically and affirmatively, and in a single day, more than two thousand people signed up to go to Bolivia.

Food for the Hungry sprang into action. Spanish classes, with additional instruction concerning orientation to life in Bolivia, were begun in Thailand. Back in Bolivia, land was cleared. Food, vehicles, and a large tractor were rushed in.

But then, about three months after the signing of the agreement, there was a major political change in Bolivia. The events that followed in the succeeding several years "would have been funny, if so much had not been at stake," Larry recounted.

Again and again, as the government in Bolivia changed nine or ten times, word came to Larry Ward to return to Bolivia to reopen contacts with the government. Each time, a new agreement was reached only to fall apart as that government was replaced by still another.

"Under any other circumstances, we would not have kept trying," Larry would reflect. "But this seemed so ideal. We could combine two problems to get one solution. Bolivia had the problem of not enough people. Thailand had the problem of too many people. It seemed to be one of those rare situations in which everyone would win and no one would lose."

But it was not to be.

After several years of arduous effort, Food for the Hungry reluctantly had to lay the project aside.

Larry would smile ruefully as he described this complicated situation. "I trust God, and I cheerfully accept the fact that this just did not work out. But I sort of hope He will explain it all to me someday! You see, our main purpose in this was to show that God always has the answers. Just as he has the answers to the problems of individuals and families, he has the answers for men and nations if they will just look to Him. This really was our bottom line. We felt that this project could be a great demonstration of how God could have an answer so simple and yet so profound that the world could not overlook it."

But overall, the effort wasn't wasted. Out of those first contacts in Bolivia on behalf of the refugees came very significant programs for the Bolivians themselves. In 1978, Food for the Hungry began a series of feeding programs in Bolivia, which in 1983 were extended to a massive scale. Bolivia had been declared one of the neediest nations in the entire world and Food for the Hungry was there to help.

Millions of pounds of food were supplied by the U.S. government, and Food for the Hungry coordinated the gargantuan feeding effort. (Food for the Hungry had previously received minor direct grants from U.S. Embassies overseas, but not from the U.S. government.)

And it all began with a refugee who cried out for help and with Larry Ward, who in turn cried out to God on his behalf.

19

"GOD DID SEND A SHIP"

FOLLOWING the major political change in Indochina in 1975, the world was suddenly awash with refugees, complicating disaster and famine conditions. The first refugees fled to the United States. A huge wave of them moved westward to Thailand. Others set off into the dangerous waters of the South China Sea on dilapidated and precariously overloaded little barks. They drifted toward Malaysia, Hong Kong, the Philippines, Singapore, and Thailand.

In 1980, after Russian troops stormed into Afghanistan, hundreds of thousands of Afghan refugees fled into Pakistan. As fighting raged in Ogaden, a disputed area between Ethiopia and Somalia became the scene of one of the world's biggest refugee crises.

Into all these areas went Larry Ward with his mission of help. His heart was especially haunted by the reports of the boat people. During the final days of South Vietnam's struggle, he had what he termed that "dubious distinction" of putting the first of the boat people into the water through "Project Noah."

Through 1976 and 1977, those little boats kept coming—first a trickle, then a giant wave.

Why?

"I could not live under the Communists," many said. Others commented over and over, "We wanted to be free." One summarized,

"My family and I had to escape from the biggest prison in the world, which is Vietnam today." They would rather risk their lives on small boats and sail into raging waves and the threats of pirates than to remain in the country of their birth.

Larry and his associates found a former Australian naval vessel—a famous ship, the S.S. *Gladstone*, with guns that had shot down the first Japanese "Zero" attack plane in World War II. It had been decommissioned from the Australian Navy, and reregistered under an aboriginal name, the *Akuna*.

The stately old convoy ship was 190 feet long and weighed over 700 metric tons. Once, its decks had known the feet of some of Australia's finest, defending their country. Now they were to feel the steps of as many as 100 to 150 Vietnamese "boat people" at a time, and sometimes to be washed by their grateful tears after they had been rescued from the rugged waters of the South China Sea.

There was an apricot glow in the eastern sky that morning of the first launch in January 1979. Through the harbor waters of Singapore, the S.S. Akuna churned northwesterly into the South China Sea, and then sailed north along the Indonesian coast. Thousands of Food for the Hungry donors had given small gifts to help. The rescue mission was on its way.

Just before coming up on deck for the early morning watch that second day out of Singapore, Larry knelt in trusting prayer on the floor of his tiny cabin. Suddenly, in his heart he felt, "a mighty surge of joy. Somehow I knew, even before I climbed to the bridge, that this was it, the day we had long awaited! Contact!"

On board the ship that fateful day were a number of students form Dr. Falwell's Liberty Baptist College (now Liberty University). One of them had been on watch, and now Larry was to relieve her. As he climbed the ladder, she shook her head disconsolately, "We haven't seen anything yet.

Larry grinned. "Stick around! We are going to see one right now." He wasn't saying it jokingly or boastfully. God had put that confidence in his heart.

He picked up the binoculars and began to scan the horizon, back and forth, back and forth.

He saw it almost immediately: a tiny boat. Dead ahead—"12 o'clock." Straining as if to extend the range of his binoculars, he could see on board what appeared to be several people. They were still, motionless, but easily discernible.

Without a word, he handed the binoculars to the first mate and pointed. As the mate focused on the little boat, slowly coming into good binocular range, his eyes opened wide, "I think so!"

The distance shortened, and still the people visible on the shallow, open boat remained silent and cautious. (Larry and his crew could not know at that hour of the cruel and inhuman piracy that had robbed the people of their food and belongings). He huddled with his interpreter-chaplain Ha Jimmy. Ha Jimmy raised his battery-operated megaphone. Across the water rang out words that almost every Vietnamese would know: *"Tin Lanh! Tin Lanh!"* ("Good News!"). This would have double meaning, for South Vietnam was dotted with little evangelical churches identified by the term *Tin Lanh*—"the 'good news' church."

Immediately the S.S. *Akuna* crew sensed the reaction. Suddenly many people were visible on the refugee boat. They had begun to move excitedly, to point, to wave.

Now, about a hundred yards away, they could hear Jimmy's full announcement in Vietnamese: "We are friends. We are Christians. We have come to help you! Do you need help? We have food, water, medicine."

By now, the little boat was wildly alive. Everyone was waving excitedly. Some held up water cans, shaking them and pointing as if to show they were empty.

"Gom on!" they cried. *"Gom on!"* ("Thank you! Thank you!")

"As long as I live, I shall remember the joy and excitement of those busy minutes which followed," Larry recalled. "We came alongside, threw down ropes, drew them closer, began to talk in a happy babble of mixed Vietnamese and English. There were eighty on board, we found, and they had been six days at sea."

In the midst of happy celebration, as the Liberty Baptist students and crew were handing out the bags of food, water, and fresh fruit, Larry's attention was drawn to one woman in particular. Her head was bowed, her face in her hands.

Concerned, he called down to her, "Are you all right?"

As she slowly lifted her head, Larry could see that her face was wet with tears. She placed her hands over her heart, as if in an instinctive gesture, and replied in English: "Oh, I am 'Tin Lanh' too! I am Christian. Seven of us on board, we are Christians."

Minutes later, after the Liberty Baptist collegians and the crew of the S.S. *Akuna* had loaded them down with food, water, fruit, little stoves, fresh milk, and vitamins, there was a quick prayer. And then the refugees were directed to a friendly shore where they could be helped in a refugee camp until there would be opportunity for resettlement in Canada, the United States, or elsewhere.

As the little boat sailed away, Larry turned to Ha Jimmy. "Just think, Jim, how those seven Christians will find their witness for Christ enhanced! Now they can remind the other eighty-one people that we helped them because we are Christians, because of the constraining love of our living Lord and Savior, Jesus Christ!"

For Larry Ward, that would have been one of life's golden moments. But there was more to the story.

A few weeks after that memorable first mission, he was back in his home in Scottsdale, Arizona, when a letter arrived from California. It came from a young lady working with the great radio ministry of Far East Broadcasting Company. She wrote, "By God's grace, my younger sister got out of Vietnam recently, and she was one of eighty-eight who you helped when they ran out of fuel, food, water." (She had seen her sister's picture in a Food for the Hungry report-advertisement in *Christianity Today*, and now a letter had come from the sister, in a refugee camp in Malaysia).

She quoted from her sister's letter: "We were waiting to die. But we prayed, and *God did send a ship* to rescue us."

Larry was at home when he read those words. He headed straight for his bedroom and fell to his knees beside his bed. His heart was full of praise to God. It had all been worth it, all the effort and strain and struggle to raise the money for the ship. (He and Lorraine had actually mortgaged their home to provide the funds for the purchase of the ship).

"Lord," he prayed gratefully, "life doesn't hold any greater privilege than this, to be part of your gracious answer to somebody's desperate prayer. Thank you, Lord, for allowing us to help."

On another day the S.S. *Akuna* arrived in Singapore with a boatload of tearfully grateful Vietnamese who had set out to sea on an inadequate boat. Hundreds of others had been rescued, but none more grateful than these. After Larry spoke to them through Ha Jimmy, one member of the group stood up to reply, "We wish we had something to give you, but we left everything behind in Vietnam and what little we had was taken away from us by the pirates. But we do want you to have this…"

And the refugee held out the compass that they had removed from their little boat before it sank. Larry took the gift and bowed. He was full of emotion and found it difficult to speak.

"I feel like another pirate to take your compass," he finally said, smiling through his tears. "But you will not need it now, for you are safe here on the deck of our ship."

Then he added: "Ha Jimmy and I have just given you another and even more important Compass, the Bible, the Word of God. You will need this special Compass as you begin your new life in America or some other part of the world. There will be problems there, problems of adjustment, problems when people do not understand you.

"Follow this Compass, the Bible. Let it lead you straight to God. Just as your compass brought you to safety of our ship, so this Compass, the Bible, can lead you to the new life found only in God through belief in Jesus Christ, his only Son."

There was an interesting sequel to all of this, actually in two parts. Larry would never forget that Christian lady whom he met in the rugged waters of the South China Sea. After their dramatic encounter, he was not to see her again until he met her with Dr. Jerry Falwell before live television cameras in the United States. What a dramatic reunion! But there was more. He learned only then that her sister, who had written from the Far East Broadcasting Company to report her sister's safe arrival in Malaysia had been one of the first fourteen people Larry had been asked to help in Saigon in 1975. She had been one of that original group for whom he launched "Project Noah"!

20

THANK GOD FOR A SENSE OF HUMOR

JUST IN FROM RUSSIA, Larry Ward hurried across a New York hotel lobby and jumped into an elevator just as its doors were closing. It was full of suitcases and people, so Larry had no room to turn around, but instead found himself pinned in, facing all the other passengers.

Somehow, the people in the elevators seemed strangely silent to Larry, and they all seemed to be wearing similar expressions of shock. Then he remembered. Perched on his head was a Russian-looking fur cap (actually from Afghanistan, where he had purchased it en route to Moscow).

As the elevator continued its slow and silent ascent, it seemed to Larry that something (*anything*, really) should be said to ease the awkwardness. Drawing himself up to his full height, clearing his throat, and looking solemnly into the faces of the other passengers, he intoned: "I suppose you're wondering why I called you all together!"

There was startled silence for just a moment, and then all the passengers burst into laughter. Larry Ward's quick wit again had asserted itself.

"Humor," Reinhold Niebuhr held, "is a prelude to faith, and laughter is the beginning of prayer." But humor is only humor when the ridiculous, ironical, surprising, or ludicrous is recognized.

Larry Ward moved easily from deep, genuine, hearty laughter to the reflective things of God and prayer.

Working in a world in which twenty-eight people starved to death every minute, constantly confronted with the heart breaking dilemmas of human need, Larry found a welcome change of pace in the humor that surrounded him on every side. He was quick to see it, eager to share it with others. In foreign lands where citizens were eager to use English, puns and non-sequiturs and awkward phrases would pop up to entertain and amuse. He quoted a road sign in Japan years ago, for example: "If a pedestrian of the foot hove in sight, tootle the horn." Or he related the cable following a dramatic answer to prayer, which was supposed to say "God reigns!" Somehow, it came out, "God resigns!"

While at *Christian Life*, he once wrote an editorial based on a sign he had seen in the deep South of the United States. It was supposed to say "Meeting Place of the United Brethren." Nothing wrong with that, but some amateur sign painter had transposed two letters and it came out, "Meeting Place of the *Untied Brethren*." Larry's editorial made the obvious point.

"Thank God for a sense of humor," Larry would say, "I think it has probably helped to keep me alive. In a miserable old world such as the one we live in, it would be pretty dismal if we couldn't enjoy a little humor. I have found that if I can make people laugh, probably no one is going to shoot me! If I act like a buffoon in the middle of the dangers, I do it on purpose much of the time. But I have to admit I also can't help it. That's my corny sense of humor."

Sometimes, it would be difficult to tell whether he thought something was funny, or whether he was quoting it just because the idea that anyone would find it humorous was so absurd. For example, riding along in a car he was suddenly apt to speak up during a lull in the conversation, to have a quick dialogue with himself:

"My sister is going to marry an Irishman." "Oh, really?" "No—O'Reilly!"

"My brother's sick." "Oh, is he?" "No, Ikey!"

Or (perhaps even worse): "Did you hear about the bird that ran into the meat grinder?" Then, without waiting for an answer, "It came out shredded tweet!"

But sometimes his humor had practical value. Customs formalities around the world always seemed to present Larry with a special challenge and opportunity to pit his skills and quick wit against oppressive bureaucracy. One time, Larry arrived in Tokyo from Saigon with a very important load of film. On the other side of the customs door stood Yasushi Taguchi, Japanese producer, waiting to pick up the film and whisk it off to a laboratory. After a call from Saigon, he had agreed to work on the film that night, and then return it to Larry in the morning, so he could carry it to the United States for use on the Today show.

But, Larry knew that he had a problem. There was nothing wrong with the film he carried, and no reason whatever why it should be detained in customs. But he was aware that a new policy had been invoked. All film coming into Japan was supposed to be inspected. This might take a full day, and Larry just didn't have that time to spend.

While he waited in the baggage claim area for his suitcase to be delivered, acutely aware of that big briefcase full of film at his feet, he entered into some friendly banter with a customs official standing behind a desk. When Larry's suitcase arrived, that man motioned for him to come to his station. As Larry lifted his suitcase and that all-important briefcase to the table, the customs officer posed the usual question: "Anything to declare?"

Looking the man squarely in the eye, Larry said with great enthusiasm: "I declare, it's great to be back in Japan!"

The Japanese broke into a great roar of appreciative laughter, turning around to explain it to his colleagues and at the same time waving Larry through.

On another occasion, Larry and two of his colleagues arrived in Bangkok form Dhaka, Bangladesh. The daughter of one of the workers there had persuaded him to carry "a bit of furniture" for her. By the time it reached the Dhaka airport to accompany him and the others in the group to Bangkok, it had grown into a full living room of wicker furniture. Again, there was nothing wrong in what Larry was doing, no customs violation. But he knew the situation well enough to know that it might be impounded, and he would have to spend all the next day trying to clear it. He didn't have that much time to spend, for he was due to leave in the early morning to go out to the refugee camps.

As his party moved up to the customs desk, Larry turned around and quickly whispered: "Whatever you do don't laugh. Give me your passports, and if the man asks you anything, just answer in Spanish or Urdu or something. Leave it totally up to me."

The customs official blinked as the three thick passports were placed together on the counter before him. "Some sort of group?"

Propping his hand behind his ear as if he couldn't quite hear the question, Larry answered: "Singapore, Tuesday!"

No matter what the official asked, Larry kept repeating those same words: "Singapore, Tuesday!"

By this time, the porters were beginning to deposit all the pieces of furniture in front of the counter. The already-bewildered official shook his head in wonderment: "What all this?"

Again Larry repeated, loudly: "Singapore, Tuesday!"

The customs official surrendered. No point talking to anyone who couldn't hear him. With a disgusted wave of the hand he sent the whole party, and all the furniture, through the door and out into the street.

The humor Larry appreciated most was not some attempt of his own to be funny, but the natural humor he saw in the situations around him.

He and a group of friends had been discussing in Japan the tendency to confuse the "L" and "R," so that "dry cleaning," for example, may come out "dly creaning."

As the three neared a museum, Larry marveled at the beautiful poster outside and the flawless English. Everything was fine, except the bottom line listing the museum hours read, "Crosed Thursday."

Larry couldn't help breaking into laughter and then was quickly embarrassed, for he didn't want to offend their Japanese friend.

"I don't mean to be rude in laughing," he said. "You speak such good English that I know you would see the humor to us in that bottom line, 'Crosed Thursday.'"

The Japanese friend looked and then began to laugh, "I get it! In United States you crose on Sundays!"

Larry was riding with his colleague Dulal Borpujari on a Thai International flight when a flight attendant paused beside them and held out a tray. Neatly rolled up, looking somehow (to Larry, at least) like a row of white sausages, were a number of hot napkins. "Oh, no," said Larry, pretending to be offended. "I tried them once, and they tasted terrible!"

The flight attendant looked quickly around, as if hoping no one had heard this stupid American. Then she bent down close to his ear and whispered politely, "Sir, they are not for eating. They are for washing the face."

"Oh, thank you," Larry said politely, surrendering on the spot.

Larry had apparently always been quick with his repartee. A high school chum recalled how his father had taken a group of Norwich High freshmen, Larry among them, to a football game at Syracuse University. As they neared the campus, the father mused, out loud and reflectively, "I wonder why it is that they always put colleges and universities on hills?" Larry responded, "Because these are institutions of *higher* learning!"

As we rode along in India one day in mid-1982, Larry was extolling the virtues of country western music. (He defended it as "pure Americana," and insisted that some of the most clever and colorful writing to be found anywhere in the early 80s was pounded out by Nashville lyricists). "All right, Larry," I challenged him, "Write us a new country western song."

Larry broke into a nasal ballad, extending his arms to illustrate the dimensions of an imaginary love, "I love her more and more each day, thar's so much more to love!"

Another time, as we drove along in downtown Bangkok, I commented both on the abundance of massage facilities and the fact that they all seemed to be labeled with the same two words, "Massage Parlor." Larry nodded and quickly came up with two new advertising slogans. One was "Rubbing Kindness" and another, "It's Nice to Feel Kneaded."

Roy Wolfe would tell of how he and Larry were at a Los Angeles Dodgers baseball game with Bob Pierce. Bob, who was also quick to note the unusual or the humorous in a situation, suddenly exclaimed: "Look, guys. Over there, three blind men coming up the stairs. I never saw a blind man at a ball game before. Why on earth would they come here?"

Larry offered the only logical explanation. "They're umpires, on their day off."

While living in Hong Kong, Larry discovered that he was allergic to the serum in which cholera vaccine is packed. His British doctor tersely warned, "Quite serious. Could be fatal."

That to Larry sounded reasonably serious, but he was traveling constantly and knew that in many countries at that time the shot was required for entrance. "Write your own," snapped the doctor. "Fake it, as you Americans say. Better that than die."

Larry decided he had better obey doctors orders, and since then administered all his own cholera shots... with a fountain pen. When I checked Larry's yellow shot record card, however, I found that even here his irrepressible humor broke through. His cholera shots bore the signature, Marcus Welby, M.D. (a fictional character from a 1980s television show).

During the last days of South Vietnam, as Dr. Garth Hunt and Larry were first beginning to launch the "exodus" in which Larry and Food for the Hungry eventually sponsored over eighteen hundred people, there were two occasions when Larry's ability to think fast saved the day.

Larry was standing at Tan Son Nhat airport, in the confusion of the evacuation center established by the U.S. military, holding his first list of sixty-two names and wondering just where to start.

Suddenly, he heard the booming voice of an American colonel asking, "Where's the special group phone?"

Larry's ears perked up. He watched as the colonel was directed to a special telephone nearby. Sliding as close as he dared, trying not to reveal that he was eavesdropping, Larry caught the drift of the man's conversation.

After the colonel had left, Larry stepped over and picked up the phone. "Ward here," he barked as soon as someone answered, trying to put as much authority as possible into his tone, "with the Food for the Hungry group."

"The *what?*"

"The Food for the Hungry group."

"I haven't heard of that one before!"

"Well, we're here," said Larry, "sixty-two of us. I've got 'em all stashed away in the old 'Dodge City' barracks." Without waiting for any further question he hurried on, "What's the procedure?"

"Well, I have to give you a number," said the other man, "You must use it when you call in every hour or so. Then I'll tell you when you are scheduled to leave, and when you should take your group out to the planes. Let's see, sixty-two of you." And then, briskly, "Okay—Food for the Hungry Special List sixty-two. F-H-S-L, sixty-two. Foxtrot hotel sierra lima sixty-two. That's your code. Got it?"

Larry had it, and that single swift action of his had probably saved hours of time trying to get official permission and perhaps, ultimately, had saved those sixty-two lives and many more.

But there was one more unexpected hurdle to cross in the hours that followed. After making numerous calls to that mysterious voice on the special group phone (Larry never did find out the other person's name), each time using the code but updating the number as his initial list of sponsorees grew, Larry finally heard the welcomed instruction, "Take your group through the last gate in thirty minutes, and then someone out on the line will put you on the right plane."

Larry rushed back to "Dodge City," anxious to share the good news with his Vietnamese friends. But as he entered the barrack, he saw gloom and alarm written all over the face of one Vietnamese man, a former official in the Saigon city government.

"It won't work," said the man. "I showed our papers to the officer at the gate and asked if they were all right, and he said 'no.'"

Oh, no, thought Larry, *worst thing he could have done*. (Larry had provided each Vietnamese family with a form he had prepared, complete with the very official-looking red seal of Food for the Hungry's Vietnamese incorporation. It wasn't exactly illegal. But it was rather unusual. It had been all he could do, though, and so far it had worked).

The gloomy Vietnamese continued, "The man at the gate said we have to have the U.S. Embassy stamp."

Larry was furious, and the Vietnamese sensed it. "Oh, Mister Larry was *so* mad with me," the man laughingly recalled to Lorraine later. "First he got red, and then he got white, and I think finally he turned green."

The man wasn't far off. Larry Ward was furious. This man's nervous "jumping the gun" might have destroyed the whole plan. This was not time to raise a question in anyone's mind. But, fortunately the officer who had expressed this negative opinion had just left, and now a big American sergeant was standing alone at the gate.

Larry recalled: "I didn't have the slightest idea what to say to the sergeant. I had the most profound respect for those American G.I.s, doing a great job at a most difficult time, and I didn't want to get him in trouble. Also, if I tried to explain and made it all sound too complicated, he would have to send for the lieutenant, and that could blow the whole thing. Believe me, I was praying!"

By faith, Larry ordered his Vietnamese group to go outside and line up, and then he walked toward the gate.

Reaching the G.I., still not knowing where to begin, Larry opened his mouth, and somehow the words tumbled out: "Sarge, I need your help. I've got ninety-four people lined up over there beside that truck in a 'column of twos.' They are ready to come through this gate, but I want to make sure I've got exactly the right number. If there are more than ninety-four, I've got some 'ringer' or 'ringers' in there who don't belong, and we don't want that, do we?"

The sergeant shook his head emphatically, "No, sir!"

"And Sarge, if there are less than ninety-four, I may be leaving somebody behind and that would be worse, wouldn't it?"

"Yes, sir, can't have that happen!"

"Sarge, will you help me count them?"

He nodded his quick assent, and then stepped out to sweep his big hand though the air and beckon the group toward the gate. "Move 'em out," he bellowed.

Staring straight ahead, for they knew how critical this moment was, Larry's little band of Vietnamese marched through the gate. As they walked past, Larry and the sergeant were counting in unison. "Two, four, six" and so on up to "eighty-eight, ninety, ninety-two and—"

"Ninety-four!" shouted the sergeant triumphantly.

"Ninety-four!" echoed Larry, tossing the G.I. a happy and very grateful salute.

And then Larry added, as the gate closed behind his greatly relieved Vietnamese friends, "I'll have other groups coming through, Sarge, some smaller, some larger."

"Will I have to count them?" asked Sarge, helpfully.

"Naw," replied Larry, "*not as long as they have these papers.*"

And he held out a sample document for the G.I. to see, complete with the red corporate seal of Food for the Hungry.

One of the members of that group of ninety-four was Ha Jimmy. He recalled: "We were all so frightened as we walked through that gate and Dr. Ward and the sergeant counted. But then we knew the Lord had helped us. So we walked around a building out of sight and formed a circle. Even the ones who were not Christians seemed to know what to do. I said, 'Let us pray,' and then I thanked the Lord of our deliverance."

Larry summed it up perfectly: "When I remember that scene, or when someone else tells about it, on the surface it sounds kind of funny. But remember, I didn't have the faintest idea of what to say. I'm not that smart. I just prayed, and then I opened my mouth and the words came out. This was another wonderful time when 'this poor man cried—and the Lord heard him!'"

21

BEYOND

HOW DO YOU sum up a life like Larry Ward's? One way is to listen to his own words.

Not long before the 1984 first publication of this book, Larry sat down in front of a video camera in the Scottsdale offices of Food for the Hungry and quietly filmed a brief message that he wanted to be played at his own funeral:

> *"I realized that this is a bit unusual," Larry began, "and I don't want to make anyone uncomfortable, or to add to the grief of those whom I have loved so much and from whom I am now separated by that grim curtain of death. But I have a very special reason for doing this, and somehow I dare to trust that you all will understand.*
>
> *Yes, I have been to a few other funerals in my life, and I recognize the natural tendency is to want to say good things about the dear departed.*
>
> *That's why I felt I should add a few words of my own, just to set the record straight.*

I have prepared another very personal tape for my dear family, so I am not particularly addressing myself to them at this time.

I just want you all to know that if there has been anything of real and lasting value in this one man's life, it's because God was there when I needed him.

I think you sense that this is a time when a man has to choose his words very carefully. He has to be 'dead-level' honest, if you will pardon the expression. And that's what I am endeavoring to do right now.

The most important thing I ever did in my life was to accept the Lord Jesus Christ as my personal Savior. He has made all the difference in my life, and I urge you, oh yes, I urge you, to come to know and trust him as I have. When you come to the end of your life, as I have now in mine, you will realize that this is the most important decision in life.

When Jesus comes into your life, you will have everything you need to prepare you for whatever comes. You'll have His Word to come alive and give you guidance, His Holy Spirit to give you the power to obey and follow the directions of this wonderful book, the Holy Bible. Yes I urge you, right now, today, even here, to accept Jesus Christ as your Lord and Savior.

And as I look back over the many years since I first came to know Him, I realize that the only things of lasting value in my life are those things, which He did.

I'm sure I disappointed Him many times in my life, but He has never disappointed me. He has never let me down.

All that I have done, through all these years and all around the world, is to cry out to Him for help. I can't take any credit, but I'm glad that I at least had sense enough to realize how much I needed Him.

I thank God for the privilege of being a hand to help the hungry, these many years. They're still out there, the hungry and hurting and homeless, but now I have to leave them with you who remain. You see, with the psalmist I now can say (using the words of Psalm 81) that I have heard the voice which said, 'Now I will relieve your shoulders of its burden; I will free your hands from their heavy tasks' (v.6). And I like the next verse, where God reminds: 'You cried to me in trouble and I saved you.'

Thank you for your kind thoughts today, and I suppose I should say thanks for the nice words that friends have wanted to say about me.

But here where I am, where truth prevails and truth is all that matters, let me sum it up in these words: 'To God be the glory; great things he has done.' 'This poor man cried and the Lord heard him!'"

AFTERWORD

THE GROWTH AND FUTURE OF FOOD FOR THE HUNGRY

THE LIFE OF Dr. Larry Ward has continued to move and inspire Food for the Hungry, its partners, and its mission. Larry's spirit has remained essential to the core values and operational structure of Food for the Hungry's calling to reach the world's most vulnerable people in the world's hardest places. The remarkable history of the organization that began with Dr. Ward continued to flourish for over forty years into an essential world mission. The following is an overview of the work that began with God's promise in response to Larry Ward's desperate prayer, "...*Father, what can I do? I'm just one person.*"

In 1984, after Dr. Ward retired, Dr. Tetsunao Yamamori became Food for the Hungry's second president. As a child, Dr. Yamamori was one of the few survivors of the U.S. bombing of the Japanese city of Nagasaki, and had first hand experience with the horrors of war and poverty. He would move the organization toward an even more global focus and emphasis on the long-term development of the people they were helping. Canadian Food for the Hungry (now FH Canada) was first registered as an official charitable organization in 1988. Korean Food for the Hungry International (KFHI) and Food for the Hungry/United Kingdom were both established in 1989.

Just as relief and development work became assimilated, physical and spiritual ministry would also be integrated in the work of Food for the Hungry. One of Dr. Yamamori's many significant contributions was his passionate and tireless championing of what he called "symbiotic ministry." The philosophy of symbiotic ministry (now called holistic ministry) has become embedded in the legacy of Food for the Hungry. Dr. Yamamori explained, "Symbiotic ministry blends evangelism (proclamation of the gospel) and social action (meeting people's physical needs) into a single, integrated, and vastly more effective effort. Symbiotic ministry implies that both evangelism and social action, though separate in function, are inseparable in relations and are both essential to the total ministry of Christ's Church."

This philosophy would become an increasingly central focus for all Food for the Hungry efforts as numerous development fields were planted and grown. Food for the Hungry began operations in Bolivia in 1978, with less than ten people. Then in 1983, when Bolivia was among the countries affected by the "El Niño" drought, Food for the Hungry/Bolivia was one of the organizations asked to participate in the relief efforts.

The early 1980s were devoted to strengthening work in Latin America while continuing to actively implement existing programs in Africa and Asia. Food for the Hungry began working in Peru in 1982 with a child development program. Activities concentrated in Lima and in the jungle area of Pucallpa. Food for the Hungry/Dominican Republic kept serving the first communities of the Dominican Republic from 1979 to 1986 through rehabilitation and development work. In 1986, Food for the Hungry/Dominican Republic expanded to the border with Haiti (Elias Piña) and to Monte Plata Province. By the mid-1980s, Food for the Hungry was actively working in many of the same areas of Latin America as they are today: Bolivia, Dominican Republic, Haiti, Guatemala, Nicaragua, and Peru.

The effects of drought, flooding, HIV/AIDS, and civil wars in eastern and southern Africa would become the next major challenges God was calling Food for the Hungry to address. Food for the Hungry expanded beyond its Kenya development work by responding to the 1984-85 Ethiopian famine. It also began implementing relief and rehabilitation programs in Mozambique, where by late 1986, over 3.5 million people faced starvation after years of conflict and drought. Food for the Hungry began relief response in 1987 and later successfully implemented two large USAID funded programs starting in 1997.

Increasingly, Food for the Hungry was learning to address many facets of poverty as the effects of human conflict were becoming more acute in sub-Saharan Africa. But few were prepared for the scale of disease that would soon decimate millions of households. This was especially evident in Uganda in the late 1980s. The organization began working in Uganda in 1987, initially as a branch of Food for the Hungry/Kenya. At that time, Uganda was addressing infrastructural and social damage wrought by thirteen years of war as well as the growing AIDS pandemic. Both AIDS and the war left high numbers of widows and orphans in their wake. These new efforts began to reveal another key principle Food for the Hungry was learning while addressing poverty: *Holistic ministry and integrated relief and development differ from nation to nation and region to region.* Addressing the felt needs of the most vulnerable requires innovative approaches and reflective strategies that are "community-based."

Throughout the early 1990s, a greater emphasis on the community began to emerge as the focus for development. At the same time, conflicts such as terrorism, genocide, and communist rebel activity were on the rise. Food for the Hungry struggled with the issues of development and conflict for a long time. In 1993, Dr. Yamamori called leaders from around the world to join together in the Dominican Republic. The result of those meetings was to agree upon a shared *"Vision of Community"* that would define the work of Food for the Hungry and the nature of community change through churches, leaders, and families. Over time, new and existing areas of operation would increasingly focus on addressing the "whole of the community" as an essential approach to serving the most vulnerable.

Food for the Hungry also began new areas of operation in Cambodia in 1990. Ten years after the mass murders in the "killing fields" devastated the country, there were still pockets of civil war and regions under the control of the Khmer Rouge. From 1975-1979, the Khmer Rouge policies led to the deaths of an estimated 2.5 million of the country's 8 million people. After a decade of such horrible attrition, infrastructure and government stability were issues. Many Cambodians who had fled the country during the previous years of war were still living in refugee camps along the Thai-Cambodian border. Food for the Hungry began relief work in these camps.

Food for the Hungry transitioned to development work in 1993 in two provinces in southern Cambodia with the Vision of Community already in mind. When this work began, there were no Christian churches located within the Food for the Hungry work area. Khmer Rouge soldiers still retained control in nearby areas. In 1994, two Food for the Hungry/Cambodia staff members were taken as hostages by the Khmer Rouge: Yim, a Cambodian staff member, and Melissa Himes (an American). The two staff members were held for a month before being released unharmed, but in poor health. Terrorism was something Food for the Hungry would encounter in several nations, but living incarnationally among community members remained central to the development ethic.

Another conflict that gained global attention in the 1990s was the Rwandan genocide of 1994. The culmination of longstanding tensions between the Tutsi and Hutu peoples led to the murder of between 800,000 and 1 million people in just 100 days of fighting. With so many dead and displaced, rebuilding the nation took years. Food for the Hungry /Rwanda served through several essential programs: Emergency Assistance for Rwandan Resettlement (EARR), The Rwanda Integrated Project for Agricultural Emergency Assistance (REPAEA) that assisted local agricultural populations to increase food security, and then RAMP (Rwanda Action Mapping Project), which was designed to help community leaders identify resources existing in each province. One of the most critical services provided by Food for the Hungry/Rwanda was the tracing and reunification of unaccompanied minors. This program helped many orphans return to the homes of surviving relatives.

The Rwandan genocide affected neighboring countries as people fled the violence. Food for the Hungry became operational in the Democratic Republic of the Congo (DRC), then called Zaire, in early 1995. The first Food for the Hungry program was in Goma in response to the Rwandan refugee crises, but quickly expanded to Uvira. The first two years of Food for the Hungry's work in the DRC was predominantly handling the thousands of unaccompanied children setting up foster-care, tracing, and re-unification programs. The Bukavu base was set up in 1997, from which current projects in eastern DRC are still run.

As the Vision of Community became more integral to Food for the Hungry work, so did the important role of the church. The Samaritan Strategy was launched in 1997 as a joint initiative of Food for the Hungry and the Harvest Foundation to envision and equip local churches to fulfill their strategic role in the transformation of communities and nations. Darrow Miller (Food for the Hungry) and Bob Moffit (Harvest Foundation) began by promoting a "school of thought" centered on the power of biblical truth for cultural transformation, the strategic role of the church in society, and the importance of holistic, incarnational ministry. Their one-week Vision Conferences were held around the world empowering FH work as well as other ministries. Today, the Disciple Nations Alliance, birthed into a separate organization, extends the work of the Samaritan Strategy far beyond Food for the Hungry operational areas of work.

Throughout the 1980s, 90s and into 21st century, Food for the Hungry was known as Food for the Hungry International (FHI) and implemented the Vision of Community in many diverse and often dangerous regions of the world. Besides those countries already mentioned, initiatives were also launched in Southeast Asia, Brazil, People's Republic of China, Honduras, Mongolia, Nepal, Romania, Tajikistan, and Uzbekistan.

These programs were facilitated by a small group of staff and missionaries in each nation, faithfully reaching out to local communities. Incarnational workers were sent out from Canada, Japan, South Korea, Switzerland, United Kingdom, and the United States. In 1998, FHI Sweden and FH Suisse (Switzerland) were added to the list of supporting nations. The ministry of Korea-America Food for the Hungry International (KAFHI) was also established in 2002 to reach the estimated 2.5 million people of Korean heritage in the United States. *After just 35 years, Food for the Hungry had grown from the vision of one man, Dr. Larry Ward, into an international organization with a global footprint of 34 countries.*

The first ten years of the 21st century would prove to be challenging, yet provide new opportunities to adapt to developing global realities. Several major emergencies were added to the ongoing issues of hunger, poverty, HIV/AIDS, and war. Dr. Ted Yamamori prepared the organization by delegating leadership responsibilities between two distinct boards: United States and international. When Dr. Yamamori retired in 2001, he named Randall Hoag President of FHI and Benjamin Homan President of Food for the Hungry (U.S.).

Food for the Hungry/South Sudan started operations in southern Sudan through Christian Aid Mission mainly in emergency relief activities in Upper Nile State due to civil war and hunger. Independent Food for the Hungry operations started in late 2004 with a staff base of three. It grew to over forty staff until a lack of funding suspended most activities in 2008. Operations were reduced in size and faced closing completely, but, by the grace of God, educational programs continued. By 2011, Food for the Hungry/South Sudan returned to around forty staff and included education as well as integrated programming including agriculture, water, health, and church strengthening.

Food for the Hungry/Indonesia was then birthed out of a need to respond to the great tragedy brought about by the massive December 2004 tsunami that claimed over 250,000 lives. Food for the Hungry's work in Indonesia began when an assessment team was sent to Aceh—near the epicenter of the earthquake that caused the tsunami. An international partnership initially responded with medicine, food, and other emergency aid, including medical teams, water and sanitation experts, counselors and other relief experts, and first responders. This later transitioned into community development work in agriculture and education. A similar pattern emerged in Africa as Food for the Hungry work in Burundi moved from relief toward development in 2007. Started as an extension office of Food for the Hungry/Rwanda, Food for the Hungry/Burundi began by focusing on agriculture, food security, and medical supply distribution.

Transitions continued in many areas of FH work beyond relief and development. Leadership and organizational structures were adjusted to better reflect existing growth and new realities. In 2006, Greg Vestri succeeded Randall Hoag as President and CEO of FHI. Later that year, Food for the Hungry leaders made an important step of moving from a "leader-led" to a "strategy-led" organization. Food for the Hungry's supporting organizations, largely in the West, made the strategic decision to closely align operations together, while those in the East decided to operate more independently.

The FH Association (FHA) was founded in 2007, with member organizations from Canada, Switzerland, Sweden, United Kingdom, and United States. Meanwhile Korean, Japanese, and independent ministries in Asia formed the FHI-Federation. While both maintained the same commitment to the Vision of Community and share a common heritage, each chose to apply different approaches to program implementation, with FHIF operating in more of a decentralized fashion and FHA working in a more integrated manner.

Early evidence for the importance of integrated work came quickly in 2010, when the largest earthquake in decades hit the poorest nation in the Western hemisphere. Food for the Hungry was already present in Haiti with child development operations along the Dominican Republic border and with HIV/AIDS and health activities in the capital, Port-au-Prince, when the quake devastated the nation. With an outpouring of response from around the world, Food for the Hungry needed to walk closely together as a global organization in order to coordinate efforts effectively with partners. Disaster response activities were quickly organized, and within a few months formed into a major development effort.

In 2012, Food for the Hungry began implementing an integrated model of development throughout all its field operations. The program model focuses on helping the world's most vulnerable children thrive as a result of community-based programs that transform communities. The model addresses the many facets of poverty faced by the most vulnerable. Specifically, programs focus on health and nutrition, food security and livelihoods, child education, and disaster risk reduction (DRR)/disaster response.

The current President/CEO of Food for the Hungry, Gary Edmonds, looks to the future with three principals in mind: first, to follow Dr. Ward's courageous example of serving the most vulnerable people, even in the most difficult places in the world. Second, to continue to pursue Food for the Hungry's ministry with the core belief that change is relational. Gary explains, "Change begins with love, trust, dignity, and respect. It is something that happens from the inside out and is never just a transferring of resources." Finally, the organization continues to be grounded in the belief born in the heart of its founder Larry Ward, that extreme poverty and distress can be changed. Gary leads Food for the Hungry with the vision of affecting the "bottom billion people in our world that suffer in extreme poverty." He maintains that the heart of the organization is still grounded in Dr. Larry Ward's love for the children who are victims of such circumstances. Gary believes that this type of poverty creates conditions for the radicalization of children that is having a major impact on today's global politics. He looks forward with the hope that Food for the Hungry can work through partnerships to significantly reduce the number of that billion people living in extreme poverty. Food for the Hungry continues to serve over 9.5 million people and is still actively working to end poverty in some of the most vulnerable areas of the world with the same convictions that God planted into the heart of its founder.

THE WHITE HOUSE
WASHINGTON

May 7, 1984

Dear Larry:

Individuals of great goodness and humanity seldom receive the recognition due them, and you are no exception. For over 25 years, you have worked tirelessly to relieve the suffering of the homeless, the hungry and the victims of disaster and war. You have created international bridges between peoples with a simple humanitarian appeal—help the poor.

Your good works, your sincerity and your consistent and constant message shine as a beacon of hope that mankind can be noble and good. There is little we can do adequately to recognize such accomplishment, but I hope you will accept my personal designation as our Honorary Ambassador to the Hungry World.

As you step down from the Presidency of Food for the Hungry International, I know it does not mean the end of your good works, for your work is obviously a way of life. You make us all proud to be fellow Americans. May God bless you and your family.

Sincerely,
Ronald Reagan

This poor man cried . . .
and the Lord heard him
and saved him
out of his troubles.

PSALM 34:6 (TLB)

He listened
and heard my cry.

PSALM 40:1 (TLB)

From the last page of
Larry Ward's Bible

For more information:

Food for the Hungry
1224 E. Washington St.
Phoenix, AZ 85034
Phone: (480) 998-3100

www.FH.org